FOCUS ON

FISHING

D1612734

AN 2575311 8

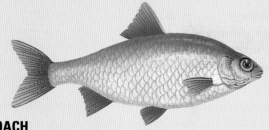

ROACH
L8-25cm, ¼-3lb.
Most fresh waters. Feeds at all depths on insects and plant pieces. Maggots on size 16 hook, casters on size 18, bread punch on size 20, redworm or bread flake on size 10-14.

RUDD
L8-25cm, ¼-2½lb.
Lakes, canals and slow-flowing rivers. Feeds on small insects and plant pieces in mid-water or on surface. Maggots or casters on size 16 hook, sweetcorn or redworm on size 12-14.

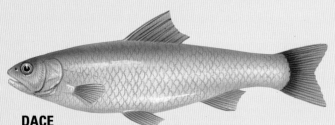

DACE
L10-25cm, 2-12oz.
Clean, flowing rivers. Feeds on insect adults and larvae. Maggot or caster on size 16 hook, bread on size 12, small wet and dry flies.

CHUB
L15-60cm, 1-6lb.
Deep pools in largish, strong-flowing rivers. Feeds on small fish, insects and worms. Worms, black slug, luncheon meat, bread crust or flake on size 6 hook.

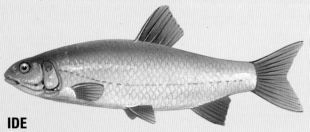

IDE
L15-60cm, 1-5lb.
Rivers with reasonable current, uncommon in UK. Feeds on small fish, insects and worms. Worms on size 4-6 hook, bread crust on size 6.

COMMON BREAM
L20-75cm, 1½-8lb.
Lakes and slow-flowing rivers. Feeds on freshwater creatures in bottom mud. Maggots or redworms on size 10-16 hook, bread or lobworms on size 8-10.

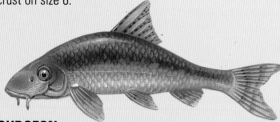

GUDGEON
L10-20cm, ½-4oz.
Rivers, canals, lakes and ponds; largest gudgeon found in gravel pits. Bottom feeder on small freshwater animals. Single maggot on size 18 hook.

PIKE
L25-100cm, 1-25lb.
Slow-flowing rivers, canals and lakes with plenty of water plants. Feeds on fish, frogs and even water birds. Deadbaits on size 10 treble hooks, and spinners, spoons and plugs.

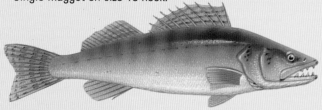

ZANDER
L25-100cm, 2-15lb.
Shallow lakes and slow-flowing, cloudy rivers. Feeds on small fish. Deadbait on size 8 treble hooks, and deeply-fished spinners, spoons and plugs.

PERCH
L10-50cm, ½-4lb.
Lakes, ponds and slow-moving rivers. Feeds on small fish. Lobworms on size 8-10 hook, smaller worms on size 10-14, small spinners.

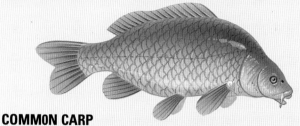

COMMON CARP
L20-55cm, 2-20lb in rivers, 2-40lb in managed lakes.
Lakes and slow-flowing rivers. Feeds on freshwater creatures
in bottom sediments. Sweetcorn or lobworm on size 6 hook,
bread crust or flake on size 4.

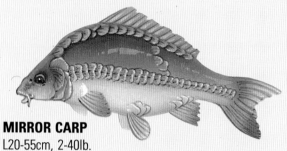

MIRROR CARP
L20-55cm, 2-40lb.
Lakes and gravel pits. Feeds on freshwater creatures in
bottom sediments. Lobworm or sweetcorn on size 6 hook,
bread crust or flake or luncheon meat on size 4.

TENCH
L20-60cm, 2-6lb.
Lakes and slow-flowing rivers. Feeds on freshwater creatures
in bottom sediments. Sweetcorn or redworm on size 14 hook,
bread flake or luncheon meat on size 10.

EEL
L40-100cm, 1-8lb.
Lowland rivers and canals, also lakes. Feeds on snails
and insect larvae. Ledgered deadbait or lobworm on size
2-4 hook.

BROWN TROUT
L15-100cm, 1-4lb wild.
Cold, gravel-bottomed rivers and lakes. Feeds on insect
larvae and freshwater shrimps. Artificial flies, spinners,
ledgered worm.

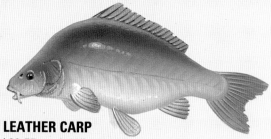

LEATHER CARP
L20-55cm, 2-40lb.
Lakes and gravel pits. Feeds on freshwater creatures in
bottom sediments. Lobworm or sweetcorn on size 6 hook,
luncheon meat, bread crust or flake on size 4.

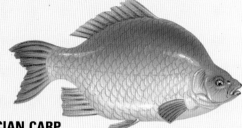

CRUCIAN CARP
L15-50cm, 2-4lb.
Lakes, ponds and gravel pits. Feeds on freshwater creatures
among water plants. Bread paste, maggot, sweetcorn or
redworm on size 12 hook.

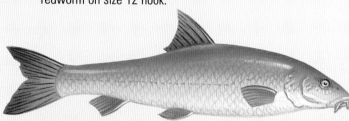

BARBEL
L15-90cm, 2-8lb.
Clear, strong-flowing rivers. Feeds on insect larvae and
freshwater molluscs on bottom. Ledgered luncheon meat on
size 6 hook, maggots on size 12.

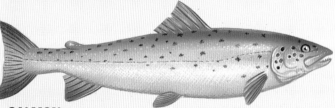

SALMON
L15-120cm, 2-25lb.
Clean, clear rivers. Feeds at sea on sandeels and small
herrings. Artificial flies, prawn, spinners and spoons,
ledgered lobworm.

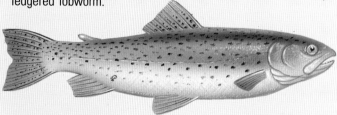

RAINBOW TROUT
L20-55cm, 1-15lb.
Trout lakes, fisheries and some rivers. Feeds on small fish,
freshwater shrimps, water beetles and insect larvae. A wide
range of artificial flies, spinners.

FOCUS ON

FISHING

TONY WHIELDON

ACKNOWLEDGEMENTS

The publishers would like to thank Kenny Collings and the staff of the Kenny Collings Angling Centre, 114 Carshalton Road, Sutton, Surrey FM1 4RL for their assistance and the loan of most of the equipment and baits for the studio photography; Farlow's of 5 Pall Mall, London SW1 for their assistance and the loan of the sea fly reel; Neil Pope, Editor of EMAP Consumer Magazines' *Improve Your Coarse Fishing* magazine, for his help with the photographs for this book; and the organizations and individuals that have supplied the photographs on the following pages:
Ardea, London/Ake Lindau 57 bottom left. Bruce Coleman Ltd/Hans Reinhard 48-49 bottom. Robert Harding Picture Library 21 bottom left. Trevor Housby 61 bottom left. *Improve Your Coarse Fishing* magazine 18 top, 42. Lefty Kreh/Hillstrom Stock Photo Inc 30 top, 75 bottom. Mike Millman Photo Services 24, 31, 52 bottom, 54 (Nigel Pinsent), 56 top and centre. NHPA/Roger Tidman 57 bottom right. Tony Oswald/Hillstrom Stock Photo Inc 8 right, 15, 30-31, 51 bottom right, 69 bottom left, 71 bottom. Reed International Books Ltd 81. Ken Schultz 28. Tony Stone Photographic Library, London/Jerald Fish 65 top left. ZEFA Picture Library, London/R. Jureit 69 bottom right.

Illustrators:
David Ashby: 11, 17 (top), 20, 21, 23, 24, 25, 27, 29, 34, 35, 36, 39, 40, 41, 43, 44, 45, 47 (top), 49, 50, 51, 52, 53, 55, 57, 58-59 (top), 59 (top), 60, 64, 66, 67, 68, 75.
Peter Bull Art Studio: 13, 15, 16-17 (bottom), 18, 19, 31, 32-33, 46 (top), 46-47 (bottom), 48, 58-59 (bottom), 65, 69, 71, 73.

Editor: Andrew Farrow
Series Designer: Anne Sharples
Designer: Mark Summersby
Picture Researcher: Liz Fowler
Production Controller: Linda Spillane

This edition first published in Great Britain 1995
by Hamlyn Children's Books.
This reprint published by Heinemann Children's Reference,
Halley Court, Jordan Hill, Oxford, OX2 8EJ,
a division of Reed Educational & Professional Publishing Ltd.

MADRID ATHENS PARIS
FLORENCE PORTSMOUTH NH CHICAGO
SAO PAULO SINGAPORE TOKYO
MELBOURNE AUCKLAND IBADAN
GABORONE JOHANNESBURG KAMPALA NAIROBI

ISBN 0 600 58787 8

A CIP catalogue record for this book is available at the British Library.

Printed in China

CONTENTS

FISHING AS A SPORT

Fishing is mentioned in several old books, but it was not until the publication of Izaak Walton's *Compleat Angler* in 1653 that it was fully discussed as a sport. His little book, full of poetic verse and charming prose, praised angling as a sport and healthy recreation - and Izaak Walton lived to the ripe old age of 90! Today, there are millions of anglers worldwide.

An angler of Walton's time. The basket is called a 'creel'.

METHODS

This book introduces you to the many exciting methods of fishing. First some basic items of equipment are described. Then there are sections on float and leger fishing for coarse fish (all freshwater fish except salmon and trout). Also covered are playing and handling fish, baits, pole fishing and fishing for predators. Next there's advice on fishing from the seashore and boats for saltwater species. Finally there are sections on fly fishing for the game fish, such as trout, sea trout and salmon.

On the following pages you will find many items of equipment described. Unfortunately, anglers and manufacturers use a mixture of Imperial and metric units. Where, for reasons of conciseness, both units cannot be shown, the unit most commonly used by anglers and manufacturers is given.

The great thrill of fishing is being out in the open air, using all your skill to hook and land a superb fish. Understand and appreciate your natural surroundings, and you will learn to be a true angler.

JOIN A CLUB

There's lots to learn about fishing. Anyone starting from scratch should spend some time quietly watching experienced anglers using their local knowledge and 'tricks of the trade'. Join a local angling club, whose address you can get from a fishing tackle shop or library. Membership of a club will also give you access to waters to fish, so it is well worthwhile!

SAFETY FIRST

Fishing is great fun, but please be sensible when near water. Always go fishing with an adult or companion, and don't go near steep, crumbly or slippery banks - find a flat, solid site. Tell an adult where you are going and when you will be back. Wherever you fish, and whichever type of fishing you decide to take up, we hope you get all the enjoyment that this sporting hobby has to offer.

Some items of tackle are fun to look at, and are works of art in their own right. This pike float, American muskellunge spinner and marabou fly-rod lure are just a few examples.

The closed-face reel (below left) and the fixed-spool reel (below right) are the types of reel most likely to be used by the beginner.

CODE OF CONDUCT

The angling code of conduct is based on consideration for the environment and other people. It is only a few stupid anglers who abuse the code - don't be one of them.

Respect plants, animals and birds.

Dispose of all litter properly.

Close all gates behind you.

Don't trample crops.

Don't disturb other anglers' swims.

FRESHWATER RODS AND REELS

The huge variety of equipment available can be very confusing for the beginner. Your local tackle dealer will be happy to help you. Start with the basics, a rod and reel. Unfortunately, no one rod is suitable for all types of fishing. Therefore it is important to choose a rod that is right for the type of fishing you intend to do. The rods and reels shown here are used for fishing for freshwater coarse fish on rivers and lakes.

FLOAT RODS
Fishing with a float rod and tackle is the ideal method to learn the basic skills of angling. The best length to start with is 10ft or 11ft (3m or 3.3m).

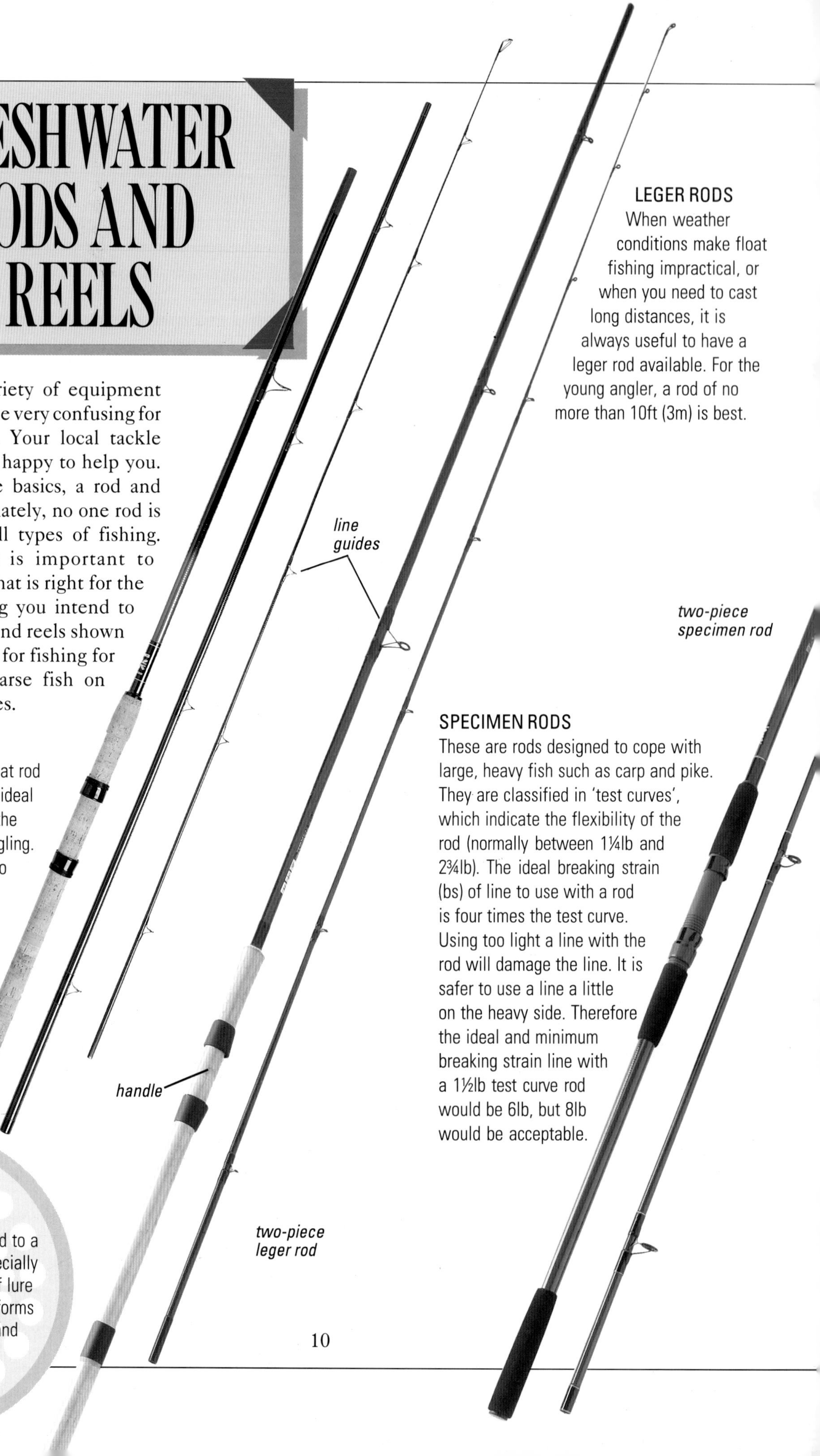

line guides

three-piece float rod

handle

two-piece leger rod

LEGER RODS
When weather conditions make float fishing impractical, or when you need to cast long distances, it is always useful to have a leger rod available. For the young angler, a rod of no more than 10ft (3m) is best.

two-piece specimen rod

SPECIMEN RODS
These are rods designed to cope with large, heavy fish such as carp and pike. They are classified in 'test curves', which indicate the flexibility of the rod (normally between 1¼lb and 2¾lb). The ideal breaking strain (bs) of line to use with a rod is four times the test curve. Using too light a line with the rod will damage the line. It is safer to use a line a little on the heavy side. Therefore the ideal and minimum breaking strain line with a 1½lb test curve rod would be 6lb, but 8lb would be acceptable.

ANGLER'S HINT
Your reel will be subjected to a lot of wear and tear, especially the constant retrieving of lure fishing. Make sure it performs smoothly by cleaning and oiling it regularly.

HOW TO LOAD A REEL

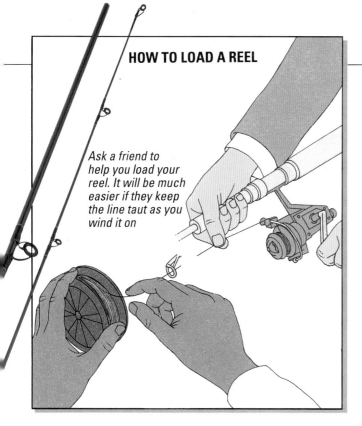

Ask a friend to help you load your reel. It will be much easier if they keep the line taut as you wind it on

TIP ACTION

Most float rods have a tip action, or bend, which is ideal for hooking fast-biting fish such as roach and dace on low breaking strain lines. They also have a mid action (a medium bend) for when the rod is subject to the greater strain of a larger fish. Therefore the ideal rod for float fishing is a 'tip- to mid-action' rod. A through-action rod is more suitable for trotting a float through swirling swims where heavier barbel or chub are present.

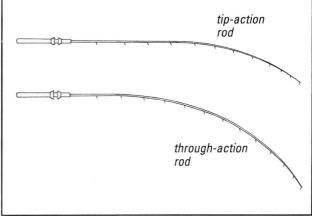

tip-action rod

through-action rod

FIXED-SPOOL REELS

Fixed-spool reels are suitable for most float and leger fishing on rivers and lakes. The line is held on a container called a spool, and is wound in via a guide called a bale. A shallow 'match' spool is preferable when float fishing with fine line, eg 2lb bs. A deeper spool will be needed for heavier line, eg 6lb bs. Spools are swapped using the release button on the front of the spool.

CLOSED-FACE REELS

When casting into the wind with a fixed-spool reel, the line will often blow back over the bale arm and create a tangle. This does not happen with the covered design of the closed-face reel. For this reason, closed-face reels are ideal for distance waggler float fishing into a wind (see page 21). However, the flow of line is more restricted than from a fixed-spool reel, which means more weight is needed to cast a particular distance. The restricted line flow can be an advantage when trotting stick floats (see pages 22-25).

bale

spool

clutch (line drag control)

spool quick-release button

handle anti-reverse switch (used to stop handle rotating backwards when striking a fish - see page 28)

bale arm

line release button

handle

LINE, HOOKS AND KNOTS

100m spool

Nylon monofilament line is available in 50m, 100m or larger bulk spools. You'll need about 100m of line for loading freshwater reels. Bulk spools of more than 100m are used mostly by sea anglers.

bulk spool

Line, hooks, floats and weights are known as tackle. Your tackle must be as light and inconspicuous as possible so that it doesn't frighten fish from the bait. On the other hand, your tackle must be strong enough to hold the fish. Fish will be more attracted to a neatly presented bait than one with odd strands of line all over the place.

LINE

A line of 2-3lb breaking strain (the weight the line can hold without breaking) is suitable for float fishing, heavier 3-4lb line is needed for legering. Choose a line that is supple and doesn't stay coiled as it comes off the spool. This coiling is known as 'memory', and means you will have less control of your float and hook.

HOOKS

The range of hooks is enormous. Sea hooks are sold in loose form, untied. Freshwater hooks can be bought already tied to nylon, or loose: you will find it easier to start with hooks already tied to line. Check the knot on shop-bought hooks connected to nylon before you use them - occasionally they are not tied or tightened properly.

It is becoming common practice to use barbless hooks, which penetrate cleanly and can be removed easily, causing less damage to the fish. Some fisheries have a 'barbless hook only' rule. You can buy barbless hooks, or squeeze a barb with forceps so that it snaps off, leaving a slight bump.

A hooklength is about 300mm of line tied to the hook. It should have a lower breaking strain than the main line so that if the hook becomes snagged and you have to break the line, only this bit of your tackle will be lost.

large bait hook

spade end hook ready tied to nylon

spade end hook *eyed hook* *barbless hook* *barbed hook*

KNOTS

It is important that you are familiar with a selection of knots before you go fishing. First practise tying them with a length or two of heavy line or string. Then practise tying them actual size, with the line you will be using.

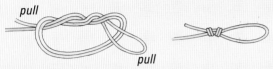

pull

pull

DOUBLE LOOP KNOT
A very useful knot for making a loop on the end of line.

hooklength

A LOOP-TO-LOOP ATTACHMENT
A very useful and easily detachable method for connecting a hooklength to the main fishing line.

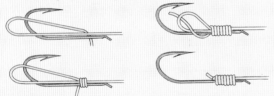

SPADE END KNOT
This knot gives a particularly neat presentation of the bait, especially with small hooks. It is well worth taking the time to master.

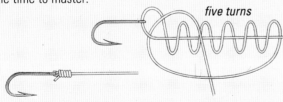

five turns

TUCKED HALF BLOOD KNOT
This is probably the most widely used knot for attaching eyed hooks, leads or swivels.

SLIDING STOP KNOT
This knot is tied on the main line when a sliding float is being used. It can be moved up or down the line to set the depth of the bait.

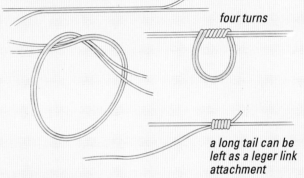

four turns

a long tail can be left as a leger link attachment

WATER KNOT
This is a first class knot for joining two lengths of line to each other.

DROPPER LOOP KNOT
Use the dropper loop knot to produce a connecting point for a paternoster (see page 60). The paternoster can be attached with a double loop knot or a half blood knot.

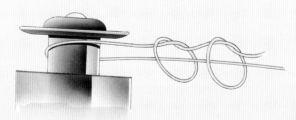

DOUBLE SLIP KNOT
Open the bale arm and use this knot to connect the main line to the reel.

ANGLER'S HINT
When tightening a knot into its final shape, ease it gently into position. Never jerk it hard, or you could damage the line. Moisten the knot just before tightening to make things slide into place more easily.

OTHER EQUIPMENT

Here is some equipment that you'll need for most forms of fishing. It's worth investing in good-quality, sturdy equipment that will stand the wear and tear of busy days by the water.

TACKLE BOX
If you don't have a seat box, this is the ideal container for holding small items of tackle.

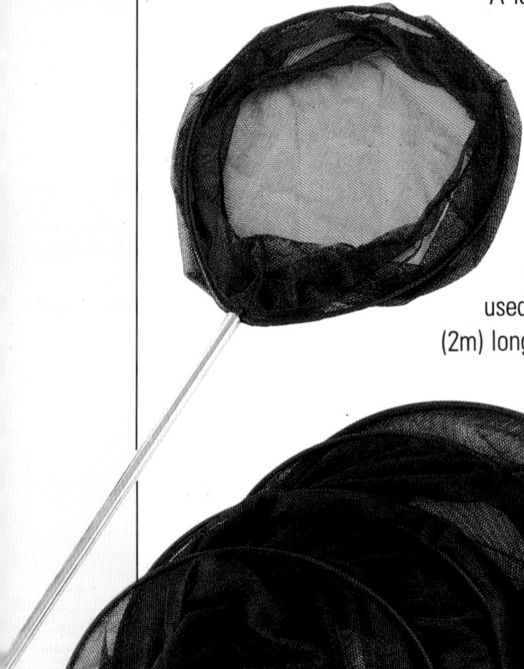

LANDING NET
A landing net is used to lift a hooked fish out of the water. This is a pan type landing net which has a diameter of 20in (0.5m) and a telescopic glass fibre handle. By law your nets must have a knotless mesh (micromesh is most widely used), and a handle at least 6½ft (2m) long.

DISGORGER
Disgorgers and forceps are essential for the quick, humane removal of hooks. *Never* go fishing without a disgorger.

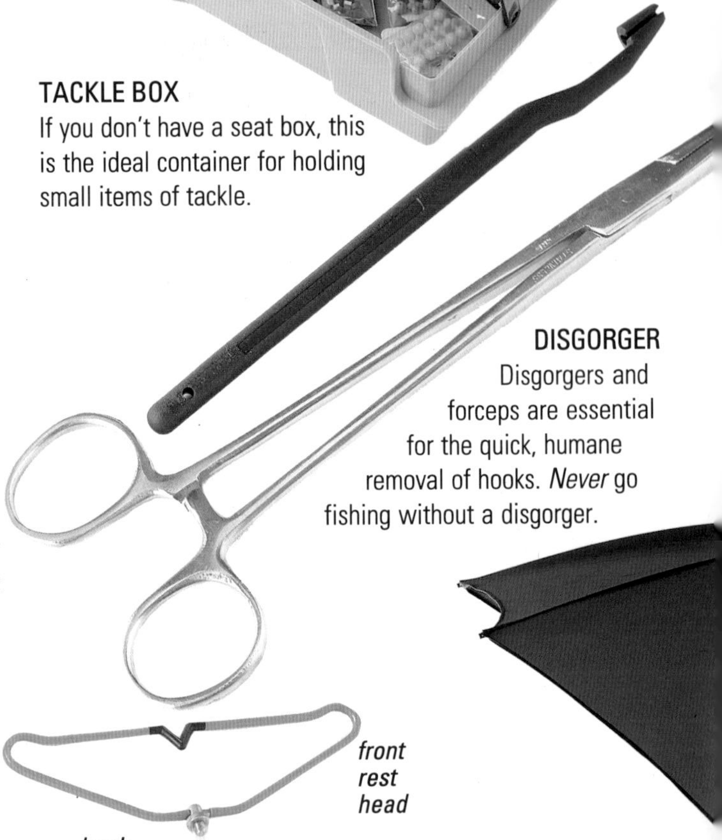

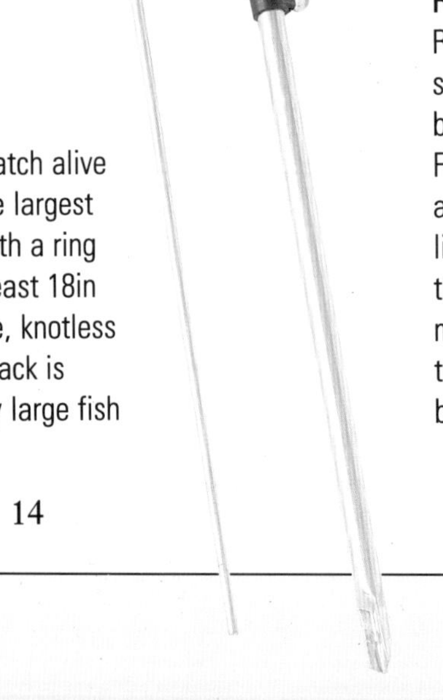

back rest

bankstick

front rest head

KEEPNET
Keepnets hold your catch alive in the water. Buy the largest you can afford, with a ring diameter of at least 18in (0.45m) and fine, knotless mesh. A keep sack is needed for very large fish such as carp.

ROD RESTS
Rod rest heads can be bought separately and attached to banksticks by a screw thread. Front rest heads should have a small 'v' in them so that the line can move freely beneath the rod. If the line cannot move freely when a large fish takes the line, your rod could be pulled off the rest.

14

USING ROD RESTS

right

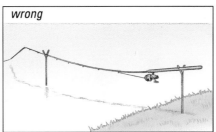

wrong

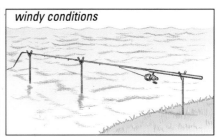

windy conditions

CARRYALL
A carryall is very useful for carrying larger items of equipment. It has a large side pocket for a keepnet.

SPRING BALANCE
A spring balance is used to weigh catches of smaller fish or individual large fish.

SEAT BOX
This serves both as a seat and a container for items of tackle.

Wear sensible clothes to go fishing. Anglers find through painful experience that short-sleeves and fishing do not go well together - stinging nettles and insects thrive near water. Insect repellant is certainly worth having to hand, especially if you are very susceptible to insect bites.

UMBRELLA
An umbrella will shelter you and your tackle from rain, wind and sun. Buy the sturdiest you can afford, especially if it's for sea fishing.

15

AT THE WATER

Before you can fish, you will need to buy a rod fishing licence. The licence, however, does not give you the right to fish anywhere - you still need the water owner's permission. The owners of most waters also have their own rules which are displayed at the fishery entrance or on the permit. Make sure you obey them, or you will be told to leave.

FISHING WATERS

The best way to get access to a fishing water is through the local angling club. Permits for club waters are usually available from tackle shops, and are often supplied with a map of all the club's waters. 'Day ticket' fisheries, where you buy a ticket to fish for just a day, are another option. Magazine 'Where to Fish' guides give locations and information on types of fish present, popular baits and cost.

SETTING UP

When you have chosen your fishing site, or swim, assemble your rod well back from the water's edge so you don't disturb the fish. If you are using a three-piece rod, connect the top two sections first. Make sure the line guides are in line before pushing the sections home. Fix the reel firmly in position, open the bale arm and thread the line through the line guides, making sure you don't miss any. Next attach your float and weights, tie a loop on the end of the main line, and connect the hooklength with a loop-to-loop attachment.

Now position your seat at the water's edge and place your gear so it is within easy reach. Keep your disgorger on a cord round your neck.

When you arrive at a water, don't start fishing in the first swim you come across. Some swims will be more likely to attract fish to feed. Scout the area and look for signs of feeding activity. When you have found a promising swim set yourself up quietly - fish can detect vibrations from clumsy footfalls. If a keepnet is permitted, stake it out before you start to fish.

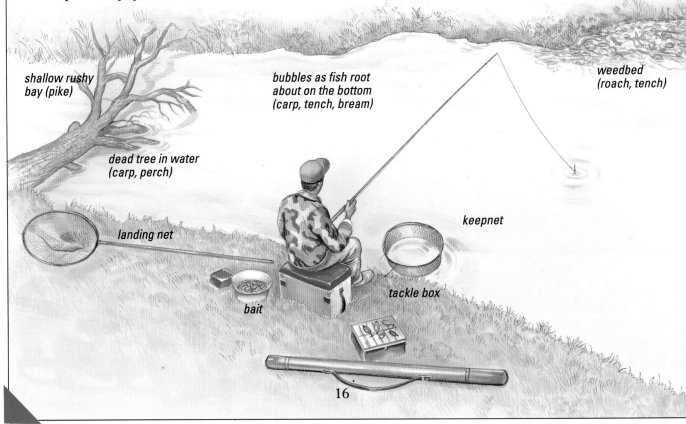

shallow rushy bay (pike)

bubbles as fish root about on the bottom (carp, tench, bream)

weedbed (roach, tench)

dead tree in water (carp, perch)

landing net

keepnet

bait

tackle box

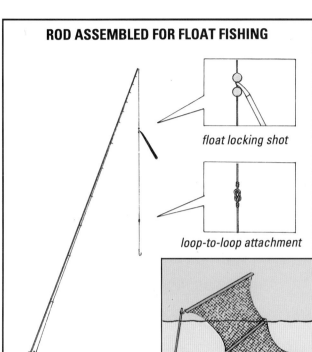

ROD ASSEMBLED FOR FLOAT FISHING

float locking shot

loop-to-loop attachment

ADJUSTING THE REEL CLUTCH

Your reel's clutch (see page 11) should be slackened off completely when it is not being used. At the start of every session, set the clutch. After threading the line through the rod guides, and before you tie on the hook, grip the end of the line with your free hand. Now lift the rod and flex the tip well over. Set the clutch so that at this point it will release line grudgingly. This means that your line will give from the reel when pulled by a large fish, and prevent the line from breaking. Never tighten the clutch right down, as this could result in the line snapping under the sharp pull of a big fish.

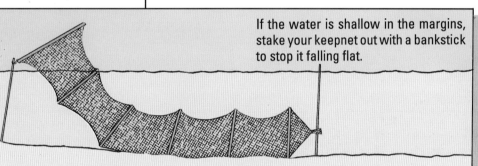

If the water is shallow in the margins, stake your keepnet out with a bankstick to stop it falling flat.

fry scattering (pike, perch or zander)

islands with overhanging trees (carp)

fish on the surface of their feeding area (roach)

lily pads (tench)

17

WARNING

There have been some very nasty accidents where anglers with carbon rods and poles have been fishing too close to overhead power lines. CARBON CONDUCTS ELECTRICITY and ELECTRICITY KILLS. Keep well clear of all electrical wires. Warning signs are displayed at some potentially dangerous spots.

HOW TO CAST

Casting is all about getting your bait out to the fish with the least disturbance. It is not difficult but needs practice and a correctly loaded reel. This section covers some basic casting techniques for float and leger fishing on both lakes and rivers.

A correctly loaded reel, positioned well up the handle for good balance and control. The line should be loaded evenly to within about 2mm of the spool edge, and the reel should be within easy reach of your forefinger. Use as light a line as possible to achieve longer casts more easily.

CASTING A FLOAT

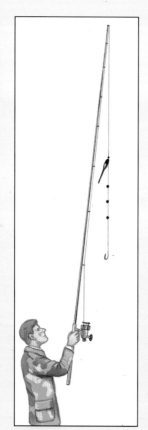

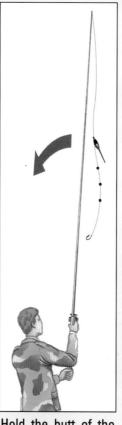

As the float and hooklength fly past the rod tip, at about 45°, release the line trapped by your forefinger.

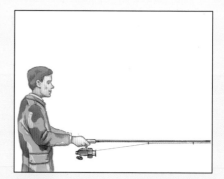

Hold the rod up and out in front of you. Trap the line against the handle with the tip of your rod hand forefinger and open the bale arm.

Hold the butt of the handle slightly away from you with your other hand. Lift the rod tip to just past the vertical.

Punch the rod forward with a smooth but positive action, keeping the butt in towards your body.

The line will spill rapidly from the spool as the tackle flies through the air. Follow through with the rod until it is about horizontal over the water. Re-engage the bale arm and wind in any slack line.

18

UNDERARM CAST

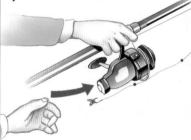

This is a simple cast for fishing close in to the bank. Trap the line with your rod hand forefinger and open the bale arm. With your other hand, hold the line just above the hook.

Swing the rod up and out over the river, letting the hook go.

As the line flies past the rod tip, release the line at the reel. The hook and shot should land gently straight out in front of you.

Trap the line with your fore-finger and close the bale arm.

HOW TO COMBAT A CROSSWIND

A wind blowing across you will have the effect of producing a bow in the line as it flies through the air. This bow can be ironed out to some extent by feathering (restraining) the line with the forefinger just before the tackle hits the water.

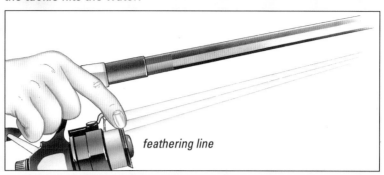

feathering line

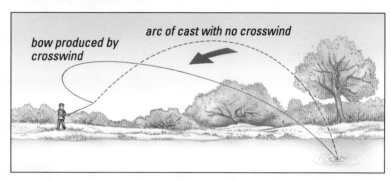

bow produced by crosswind

arc of cast with no crosswind

CASTING A LEGER

The basic method of casting a float also applies for leger fishing (see pages 38-41), although you should use a lazier action. The heavier tackle used will give a longer cast, but you will also get a larger wind bow in the line (see above) because there's more line airborne.

USING A MARKER

Accuracy is very important, especially for placing your bait in a groundbaited area. Aim at a feature on the far bank, such as a tree.

FLOAT FISHING IN STILL WATER

Float fishing uses a float to signal that a fish is taking your bait. For float fishing on a still water, such as a lake or reservoir, you should set up your equipment and tackle as described on pages 16-17. You now need to find the water's depth, using a heavy weight called a plummet, which is clipped on to the hook.

Floats for stillwater fishing, called waggler floats, are made with a variety of materials including peacock quill, sarkandas reed and balsa wood. Some, called loaded wagglers, have a weighted base. This permits a longer cast while allowing light shotting (see page 22) to be used further down the line. Only the top 20mm of the float, the coloured tip, should show above the water.

PLUMBING THE DEPTH

Although a plummet may scare fish already in the swim, it will help you to place your bait on or near the bottom, where most fish feed. Estimate the depth of the water and set the float at that depth. With the bale arm open and the line trapped by your forefinger, lob the plummet out in a smooth underarm swing, releasing the line as you would when casting. Leave the bale arm open until everything has settled and the float is hovering directly over the plummet. Reel in and, if necessary, adjust the position of the float until it stands at the correct depth in the water.

Now you can remove the plummet, bait your hook and cast out to catch some fish.

PLUMBING THE DEPTH

float set too shallow *float set too deep* *float set correctly*

FLOATS

For stillwater fishing, three types of float, called insert, straight and bodied 'wagglers', are used. The bottom of the float is attached to the line and locked in position by two or more small shot, or weights. These 'locking shot' also provide casting weight. It is best, unless fishing very close to the bank, to have at least two-thirds of the weight as locking shot.

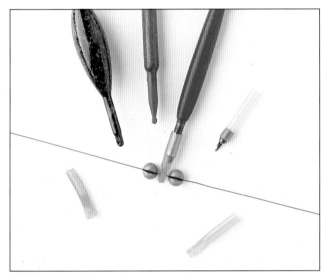

Quick change float adaptors (above). Floats can be changed without having to reassemble the whole rig.

Concentration is essential when float fishing, as the two young anglers (below) are demonstrating.

STILL WATER RIGS

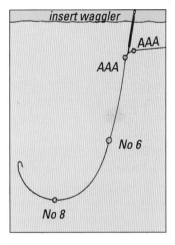

insert waggler
AAA
AAA
No 6
No 8

Insert wagglers are very sensitive floats but need calm conditions. This is a light insert waggler rig for fishing at close range or 'on-the-drop'. Because most of the shot (see page 22) is placed near to the float, the bait falls slowly to the bottom. This may tempt fish, such as roach and rudd, that sometimes feed well off the bottom.

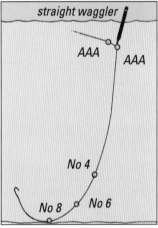

straight waggler
AAA
AAA
No 4
No 8   No 6

Use a straight waggler when the surface of the water is drifting strongly. Placing heavier shot near the bottom of the rig helps to hold the bait down.

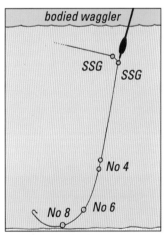

bodied waggler
SSG
SSG
No 4
No 8   No 6

This bodied waggler rig has an arrangement of heavier shot for making longer casts and casts into the wind. The bodied waggler's long, thin stem is barely affected by surface drift on the water.

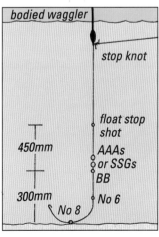

bodied waggler
stop knot
float stop shot
450mm
AAAs or SSGs
BB
300mm   No 6
No 8

This is a rig for deep water. When fishing in very deep water, locking shot can't be used because the rig is too long to cast. Therefore a stop knot is used to stop the float at the correct depth, and the shot is aranged close together, or 'bulked', further down the line. A heavy shot load is needed for long casts into deep water.

SHOT

Weights, called shot, are needed to cast the float and bait and to set the float correctly. There are many types of non-toxic shot available. They come in the same size ratings as the now illegal toxic lead shot: SSG, AAA, BB, No 1, No 4, No 6 and No 8 - the larger the number, the smaller the shot. There are some other sizes available, but those listed above will be fine to start with. The larger sizes - SSG, AAA and sometimes BB - are used mostly as locking shot, while smaller ones are spread down the line. If shot have to be bunched together - to combat surface drift, for example - they are referred to as bulk shot.

The amount of shot needed to set a float properly is marked on the float's body. As a rule of thumb, 1 BB = 2 No 4s = 4 No 6s = 8 No 8s. Shot should be squeezed firmly on the line. Don't slide them along the line, which will damage it; prise them open with your fingernail and reposition them.

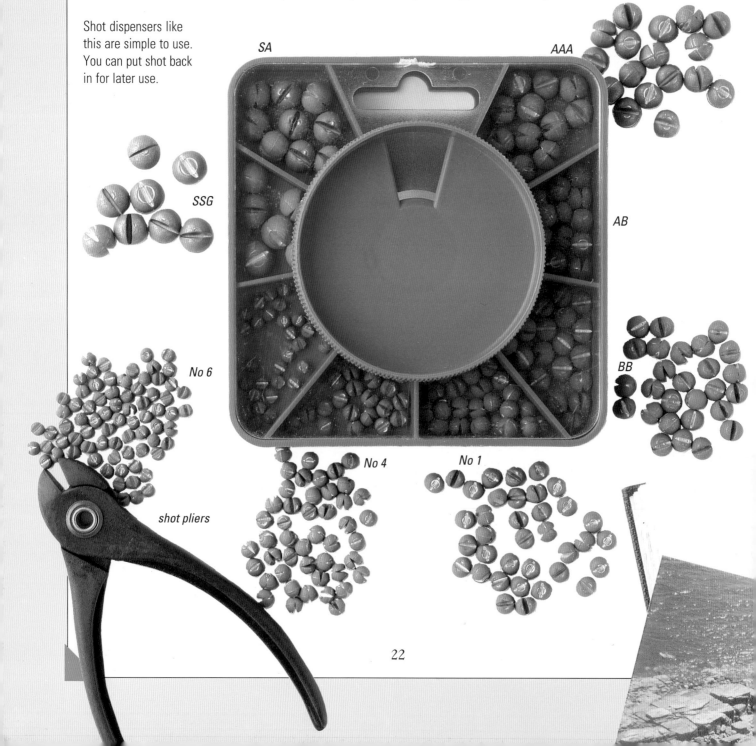

Shot dispensers like this are simple to use. You can put shot back in for later use.

SA

AAA

SSG

AB

No 6

BB

shot pliers

No 4

No 1

SINKING THE LINE

More often than not, the surface layer of water will tend to move in the wind, creating a bow in the line and dragging the float out of the feed area. In bad drag conditions, with the bottom shot on the lake bed, the tip of a light insert float could even be dragged under the surface. Avoid problems with the wind by sinking the line beneath the surface.

Cast some distance beyond the feed area.

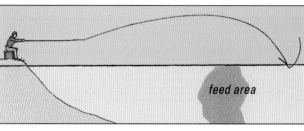

feed area

Sink the rod tip beneath the surface.

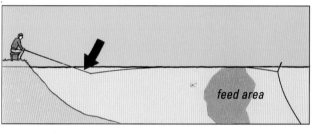

feed area

Reel in until the tackle is over the feed area.

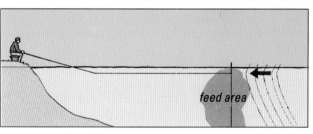

feed area

KEEPING A RECORD

Having found the depth of the water, keep a record of its depth for the next time you visit. You may need to take account of seasonal variations in the water level. There's no need to measure your line - just make a note of the number of rod line guides from the float to the hook. If the depth varies across the lake, use features on the far bank as a guide to direction - if you fish from the same spot you can use them as aiming points.

Why not keep a log book of all your outings? Note the day, time, exact location and weather, and also the details of the tackle and baits you have success with. This will help you learn the best rigs, locations and circumstances in which to fish. You can also stick in photos of your best catches.

It can be very useful - and enjoyable - to look back on a well-kept log of your previous fishing outings.

Location	Date	Hours	Weather	Roach	Rudd	Dace	Chub	Tench	Bream	Carp	Perch	Notes
e Ford, River t (just above e weir)	4/7 2pm	2	Warm but overcast, light breeze	1½lb +3								1lb

FLOAT FISHING IN RIVERS

The best method of float fishing in moving water is called 'trotting'. The float is cast into the current and the bale arm is left open so that the line can be pulled from the spool. The float is then allowed to run downstream with the current, presenting the bait to the fish in as natural a way as possible.

READY TO TROT

There's no need to use a plummet to find the depth of a swim - indeed, it could frighten any fish already there. Instead, set the float at the estimated depth of the swim and make a practice trot. If the float travels through the swim freely, move it up the line and trot it downstream again. When the float falters occasionally on a run, that shows you have the correct setting, with the·bait just off the bottom.

Although fixed-spool reels can be used for trotting, a closed-face reel is more effective as it does not spill line so readily. If you are using a fixed-spool reel when your bait is taken, trap the line with your finger and strike (lift the rod firmly) to hook the fish. Immediately engage the bale arm with a quick turn of the handle, then play the fish (see pages 30-32).

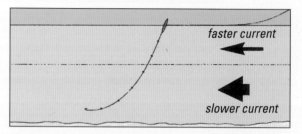

CONTROLLING THE BAIT

faster current

slower current

This is the correct arrangement of trotted float tackle as it makes its way downstream, with the hookbait and shotting always ahead of the float. Use your finger to check the line slightly at the reel, so the hookbait precedes the float.

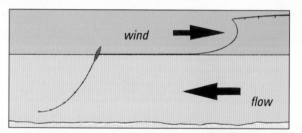

wind

flow

The ideal condition for trotting is when the wind is blowing upstream. This holds back the float so that the hookbait precedes it downstream.

You'll have to watch and control your tackle constantly as it moves downstream. It is easiest to trot when the fish are directly downstream of the rod tip. If the area you want your float to trot through is further out than the length of your rod, lob the tackle out with a smooth underarm cast.

CONTROLLING THE FLOAT

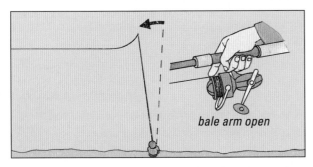

bale arm open

Follow the float with the rod tip, a fraction slower than the speed of the surface water, with your finger trapping the line.

Lift your finger from the spool and move the rod briskly away from the float. Line will come off the reel. Retrap the line and repeat the procedure.

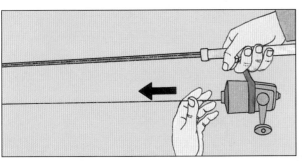

The slightly restricted line flow from a closed-face reel makes it ideal for trotting a float. Some control of the line, using your free hand, may be needed occasionally.

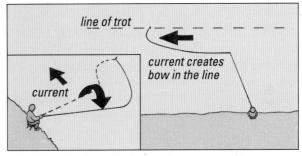

line of trot

current creates bow in the line

current

If the line of the trot is beyond the rod tip, the current may produce a bow in the line, dragging the float off course. This can be cured by trapping the line at the reel and simply lifting it over with the rod.

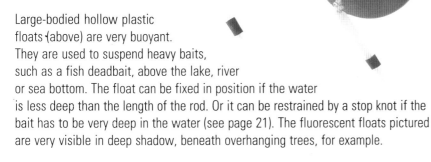

Bubble floats (below right) are used for providing casting weight for small, light baits. The required weight is created by putting water into the body of the float through a filler cap. Some bubbles are transparent and excellent for stillwater fishing, others are brightly-coloured for good visibility.

Large-bodied hollow plastic floats (above) are very buoyant. They are used to suspend heavy baits, such as a fish deadbait, above the lake, river or sea bottom. The float can be fixed in position if the water is less deep than the length of the rod. Or it can be restrained by a stop knot if the bait has to be very deep in the water (see page 21). The fluorescent floats pictured are very visible in deep shadow, beneath overhanging trees, for example.

ANGLER'S HINT
After each trot downstream, the tackle should be retrieved *away* from the fishing area. If you pull the tackle through the fishing area, the fish may be frightened away.

STICK FLOATS

Whereas the same rod can be used on both still and moving waters, different floats will be needed. Stick floats are the lightweights of the river. They are ideal for fishing smooth, medium-paced swims, about 1.3m deep, where dace and roach are the quarry. Avon floats are the best for long trotting in steady runs - the sight tip is very visible at long distance.

BALSAS

Balsa floats come into their own when the river is running slightly higher than normal and the swim takes on a swirling look. It will pay to have a variety of sizes in balsas, from a small size no larger than a stick float to the giant of the balsa range called a chubber. This 'big daddy' of river floats is designed to carry large baits such as luncheon meat, bread flake or lobworm through rough, deep swims where big chub and barbel are expected.

WIRE-STEMMED FLOATS

Wire-stemmed stickfloats and Avons are more stable in the water because of the extra weight of the stem. Thus they are the ideal floats for you to use until you become more skilled at trotting with lighter sticks and Avons.

FLOATING LINE

When fishing these floats, the line from the rod to the float should never be allowed to sink. Some monofilament lines float quite readily. A tackle dealer will advise you which brands do this. Alternatively, you can rub or spray on a chemical, called floatant, that will make the line float.

Stick floats, balsas and Avons are connected to the line with two float rubbers, one near the top of the float and one at the bottom.

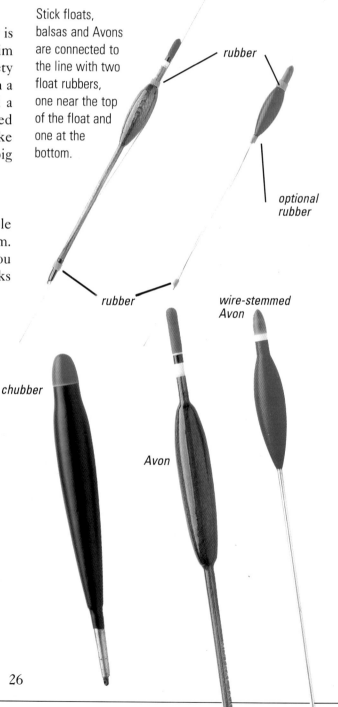

rubber

rubber

optional rubber

wire-stemmed Avon

Avon

chubber

balsa

wire-stemmed stick

standard stick

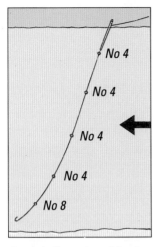

A stick float rig with shot spread evenly down the line works well in slowly-flowing water.

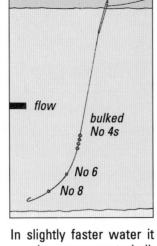

In slightly faster water it may be necessary to bulk the shot nearer the hook to keep the bait down.

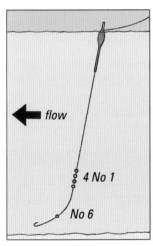

Avon floats, designed for long, streamy runs, are usually fished with shot bulked well down the line.

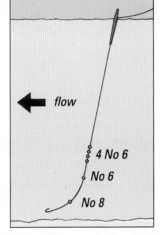

Balsa floats are also best fished with the shotting bulked. They are a good alternative to stick floats when the water is running higher than normal.

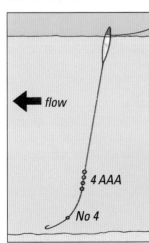

Chubber floats are very buoyant and can carry a large amount of bulk shot in very rough water conditions.

SNAGS

When trotting the stream, there's always a risk of snagging your line on an underwater obstruction. If you know the position of an obstruction, hold the float back harder than normal so that the hookbait will swing up and over it.

Having an intimate knowledge of a swim certainly helps to avoid snags. Take a look at the swim when the river is running low and clear on a bright sunny day. Wear polarised sunglasses, which cut out the surface glare and allow you to see objects under the water. Most bottom features will be visible in these conditions.

If it has been raining hard and the river level is high, try casting into slack areas. Fish often move close to the bank to avoid excessively strong currents.

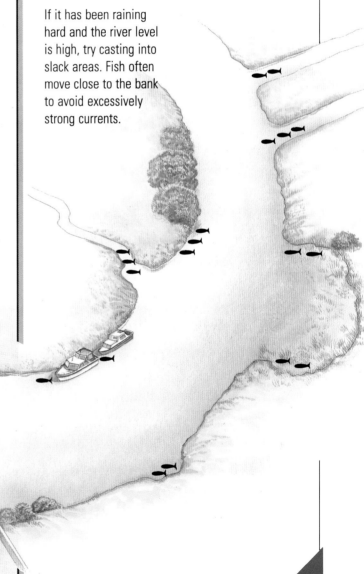

BITES

Bites indicate that fish are interested in your bait. They are quite varied. Some species of fish feed in a delicate manner, sucking or mouthing the bait before eventually taking it in a more positive manner. Others will literally grab it and run.

BITES ON FLOAT TACKLE

The type of movement of a float will often show which species is at the end of the line. If you can interpret these float signals, building up a mental picture of what is happening beneath the water, you will be able to respond at the right time and hook the fish in a proper manner.

THE STRIKE

The point at which you lift the rod and hook the fish is known as the strike. Your strike should be firm and positive so it takes up any slack line and sets the hook, but not so hard that the hook is ripped out of the fish's mouth.

A correctly-hooked fish should have the point of the hook embedded in the mouth area, where it is easy to remove, either by hand or with a disgorger. A badly-hooked fish (one which has taken the bait deeply into its gullet) is usually the result of an inattentive angler. Therefore pay constant attention to the float or bite indicator while the bait is in the water. If you have to move away from the swim, even for a few moments, wind in your tackle, and re-cast when you return.

A predator snapping at a spinner or plug (see page 50) will hook itself. Usually the hook or hooks will be caught in the front part of the jaw, as with this North American walleye. This means the fish can be unhooked cleanly and quickly.

BITES

LIFT BITE

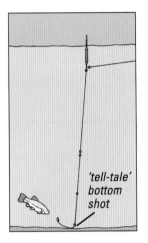

This is a common type of bite, by fish such as tench, bream or larger roach, when a bait is fished on the bottom.

'tell-tale' bottom shot

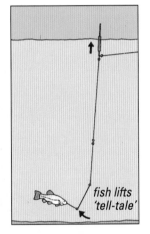

The fish takes the bait and rises off the bottom, taking the bottom shot with it. The float rises immediately. Strike at this point to hook the fish cleanly.

fish lifts 'tell-tale'

A VARIETY OF BITES

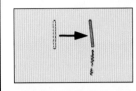

Sometimes the float will start to move along the surface. Strike immediately, in the opposite direction to the float movement.

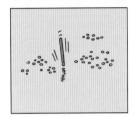

When fish are rooting on the bottom of your swim, the float will often dither and bob as fish bump into the bait. Don't strike until the float moves positively.

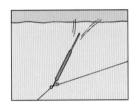

There is no mistaking this sailaway bite. Sometimes the float will dart under very quickly, at others it will sink slowly beneath the surface. Strike immediately!

PIKE AND ZANDER BITES

When pike or zander take a fish bait, the float moves away and under very positively. It used to be accepted practice to let the fish take the bait well into its mouth before striking. This resulted in many deeply-hooked fish. Nowadays, thankfully, this is frowned upon and you should strike immediately to set the hook in the mouth area.

ON-THE-DROP BITE

After the cast, the float will settle lower and lower (see bottom diagram) as each shot settles into position. Any break in this sequence will probably mean that a fish has taken the bait. This is the time to strike. Roach and rudd respond particularly well to this method.

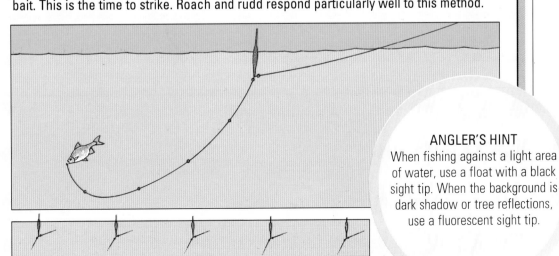

ANGLER'S HINT
When fishing against a light area of water, use a float with a black sight tip. When the background is dark shadow or tree reflections, use a fluorescent sight tip.

LANDING AND HANDLING

It takes skill to land, or bring in, a large specimen. Imagine that you are fishing a lake that contains large tench. Your reel is loaded with 4lb main line, attached to a hook length of 3lb, which in turn is whipped to a size 14 hook baited with a single grain of sweetcorn. Soon you see clouds of fine bubbles on the surface. The tench are moving in...

BATTLE COMMENCES

Suddenly the float is gone. On lifting the rod to strike, you feel the solid resistance of a big fish - 5lb at least! It is hooked and tries to escape. It makes a long run away from you, taking line off the spool against the resistance of the reel clutch. There's no doubt you've hooked a real fighter!

You can't just reel it in, because it's too strong for your tackle. So you apply a little extra pressure to the spool with your forefinger. This restrains the line, causing the fish to change course - veering towards a large bed of water lilies! If it reaches them the line will snag in the stems, and the fish will be lost!

PLAYING THE FISH

So far you have been holding the rod well up, using its flexibility as a shock absorber. Now you must quickly lay the rod over to the left, finger still on the spool, in an attempt to turn the fish away from the snag. Under your skilful control, it veers away.

When the fish shows signs of tiring, recover line by lowering the rod into the fish, winding in line as you do so. Use the rod as a lever to pull the fish towards you, then lower the rod again and wind in more line. Be prepared for the fish suddenly regaining a second wind and making long, powerful runs. If the fish heads towards you, raise the rod high and wind in line quickly - the fish could come off the hook if the line goes slack.

HOW TO PLAY A FISH

Use a firm, steady pumping action to recover line. Always keep the rod tip high when playing a big fish. *Never* point the rod directly at the fish.

Pull the rod up, using its action to gain line.

Let the rod out to the fish, winding in the gained line.

Repeat the process, easing back the rod to gain line.

Apply side strain to turn a fish away from a snag.

A critical time when playing a fish is when it is being drawn to the net (left). A fish will often find a reserve of energy and make a powerful run. If you are not prepared for this sudden surge, it could snap your line or pull the hook free.

To land very small fish, hold the rod at about 45°, and reel in. When the length of line from the rod tip to the fish is the same as the rod, lift the fish from the water and swing it in to your hand. This young angler has wound in too much line.

INTO THE NET

After a spirited battle your fish tires and circles under the rod tip. You reach for the landing net. You hold the net still, the rim just beneath the surface, and bring the fish over it. You lift the rim of the net clear of the water, and have your prize!

UNHOOKING

Once caught, the fish must be unhooked. Lay down your rod, and with both hands slide the net towards you. The fish should be perfectly hooked, just inside the top lip, so that a nudge with a disgorger will have the hook out in a second. You may want to transfer the fish to your keepnet to weigh it later, or put it straight back into the lake.

If you believe you have caught a record fish, find witnesses to your catch and take a photo of it. Write down all the details of the catch - time, location, weight of fish, how it was caught, and the names and addresses of any witnesses - and submit them to the local club.

HOW TO HANDLE FISH

Wet your hands before handling a fish. This is because fish are covered in a coating of protective slime, which will stick to dry hands. If a fish loses this protective coating, it will be more susceptible to infection and disease.

Small fish can be held in the hand to have the hook removed. Larger fish should be laid on a soft, damp surface. Use forceps for removing hooks from sharp-toothed pike or zander.

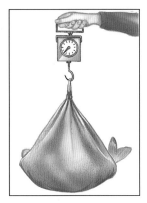

Use a weighing sling when weighing your catch. Never weigh a fish by the gills if you intend to return it to the water. Most owners have a rule that all coarse fish must be returned alive to their river or lake.

Hold large fish upright in the water until they can swim away of their own accord.

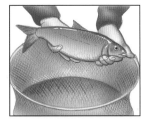

Place fish gently into a keepnet - do not drop them in. Never put too many fish in a keepnet.

Very large carp should never be kept in keepnets. Keep sacks are far better.

When releasing fish from a keepnet, hold the net and let the fish swim out.

UNHOOKING A PIKE

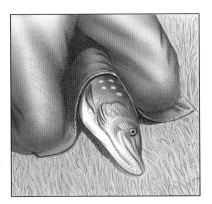

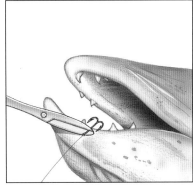

Be firm but gentle when unhooking large predators. Lay the fish on its side on a soft, damp base or grass. Kneel astride but not on the fish. Wear a soft gardening-type glove on one hand.

Now slide your gloved forefinger beneath the fish's gill cover and forward towards the front of the jaw. Lift the pike's head just off the ground and its mouth will open. A pike can also be carried like this.

Use forceps or long-nosed pliers to remove the hooks, gripping them by their shanks. Small-barbed or barbless treble hooks are easiest to remove.

USING A DISGORGER
Keeping the line taught, slide the disgorger down the line until you feel the resistance of the hook. Give a slight push and the hook will come free. Don't use too much force. If you can't free a hook, cut the line as close to it as possible - the hook will probably rust away or pass through the fish.

BAITS

There isn't one 'magical' bait that will catch a fish on any occasion, so carry a selection in case your favourite one isn't working. The baits shown here are just a few used by anglers, and you can experiment with others. Many baits, such as maggots and groundbait mixes, can be bought from tackle shops.

MAGGOTS
Large whites are the most widely used maggots. Pinkies and squatts are much smaller maggots which make good loose feed (see page 36) and also good hookbait when fishing with very fine tackle. If you are not using them immediately, store maggots in a cool place to prevent them turning into casters.

CASTERS
If maggots are left they will turn into casters. If left longer still, an adult fly will emerge from each chrysalis. However, it is the point where they have freshly turned from maggots and are a golden amber colour that casters are most effective.

hook buried

hook protruding

BREAD CRUST AND FLAKE
Bread crust is a very buoyant bait, ideally suited to surface fishing for carp or for fishing over a layer of bottom weed. Flake is an excellent bait for chub, large roach, carp and tench.

large whites

pinkies

squatts

bread crust

PREPARING BREAD PASTE

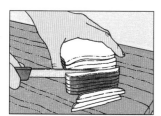

Remove the crust from a stale sliced white loaf of bread.

Soak the slices in some cold water until they are soggy but not breaking up.

Wrap the slices in a clean cloth and squeeze them to remove excess water.

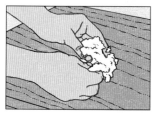

Knead the bread until it becomes a firm, smooth but non-sticky paste.

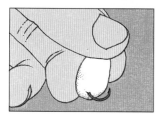

Mould the paste right around the hook, leaving the point exposed.

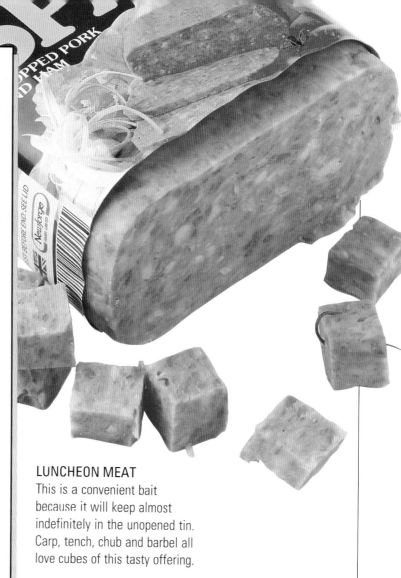

LUNCHEON MEAT

This is a convenient bait because it will keep almost indefinitely in the unopened tin. Carp, tench, chub and barbel all love cubes of this tasty offering.

PUNCH AND PASTE

Bread punch is an ideal canal roach bait and is named after the tool which is used to cut out a small piece from a slice of bread and transfer it to the hook. Paste is made by mixing bread with water. Some anglers flavour it with honey.

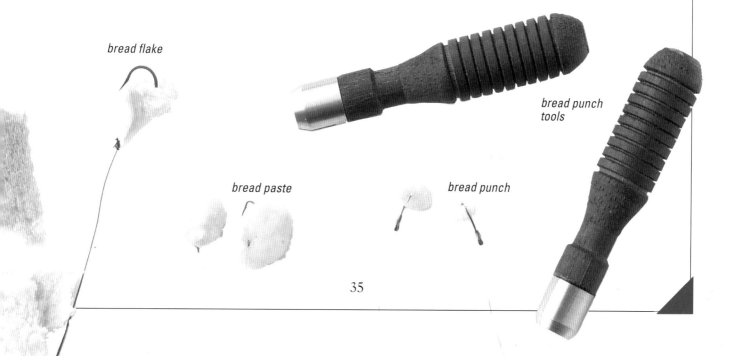

bread flake

bread paste

bread punch

bread punch tools

GROUNDBAIT

When fishing for bottom feeding fish, a swim can be brought to life by introducing groundbait before you start. The idea is to attract the fish into the swim and keep them interested, but not satisfy their appetite so they ignore the hookbait.

LOOSE FEED

Loose feed is simply a number of free hookbait samples introduced to the swim by hand or catapult, to keep the fish in your swim. Loose feed can be used after the groundbait has gone in or as an alternative to groundbait.

GROUNDBAIT

A good basic ingredient for groundbait is dry mixed brown and white bread crumb. Samples of the hookbait can be mixed with the groundbait before it is put into the swim. The groundbait mix is rolled into balls and thrown by hand into the swim. A groundbait catapult can also be used, especially when fishing at longer ranges.

MIXING GROUNDBAIT

Mix groundbait at the waterside before you assemble your fishing gear. Add some river water to a generous amount of crumb. Knead well with both hands, adding more water if necessary, until the mix can be formed into balls.

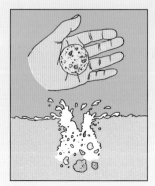

When you've set up your tackle, throw several golfball-sized balls into the area you intend to fish. The groundbait balls will break on impact.

It is worth groundbaiting a couple of areas - you can alternate between them during the session. You should also keep some groundbait for use later in the day. Store it in a cool, shady position so it doesn't dry out.

lobworms

LOBWORMS

Lobworms can grow very large, and make an ideal bait for carp and large perch. They can be collected from the surface of a damp lawn, after dark, when they emerge from their holes. Pop them into a ventilated container lined with damp moss where they will scour themselves clean. Don't put them in soil - they'll create a slimy mess.

redworms

REDWORMS

Redworms are lively worms that can be found in compost and well-rotted manure, or under leaf mould. Use small ones of about 25mm in length for roach, and 50mm ones for bream and tench. You can make your own redworm trap by placing a wet sack on damp, shaded ground.

BRANDLINGS

These are like redworms but have light body rings. They can be found in manure heaps. Unfortunately for anglers they have a very pungent smell, though this doesn't seem to bother the fish.

brandlings

CHEESE

Cheese should, be considered a fun bait, one to experiment with when not much else is working. There is no denying it is capable of attracting fish, though - some anglers use nothing else. Mix it into some bread paste, as cheese on its own tends to harden when immersed in water.

TINNED SWEETCORN

Not many fish can resist this delicacy. For safety and convenience, open the tin at home and transfer the pieces to a plastic bait box.

LEGERING

If the fish are feeding a long way out from the bank, or the wind is too strong for a float, it is time to try legering. This method uses only a heavy weight to hold the bait near the bottom, and a bite indicator on the rod. This method should not be regarded as a standby or last resort, though, for many specimen hunters use legering all the time.

The basic leger rig is the freeline, where the baited hook is the only weight on the line. To cast light baits any distance, however, some weight must be added. Most weights are attached to a link - a length of nylon - so that when the fish takes the bait the bite will register on an indicator before the fish feels the resistance of the weight and drops the bait.

LEGER WEIGHTS

Large freshwater leger weights are called bombs. They incorporate a swivel, half of which is moulded into the top of the bomb, the other half exposed. Another type of bomb, the screw bomb, has a screw-on swivel. This means that the bomb can be changed without breaking down the rest of the rig.

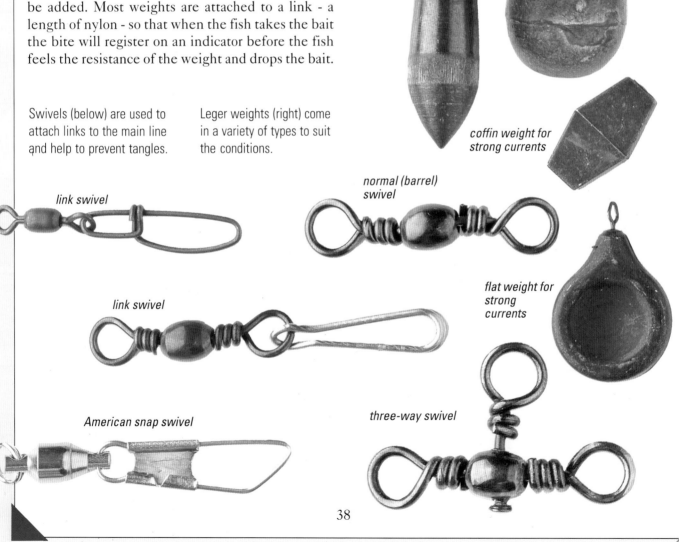

Swivels (below) are used to attach links to the main line and help to prevent tangles.

Leger weights (right) come in a variety of types to suit the conditions.

screw bomb

bomb

coffin weight for strong currents

link swivel

normal (barrel) swivel

link swivel

flat weight for strong currents

American snap swivel

three-way swivel

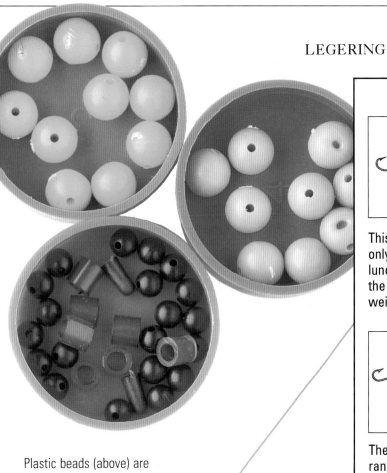

Plastic beads (above) are useful as a buffer on a sliding leger rig (below).

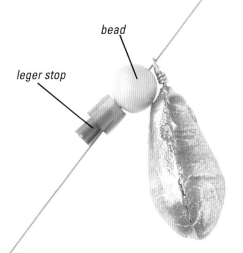

bead

leger stop

Leger stops (above) are anchor points for leger weights. They are much kinder to the line than split shot and can be used time and time again. Keep a good supply in your box, though, because they are easily lost.

LEGER RIGS

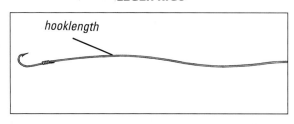

hooklength

This basic freeline leger rig is very sensitive, but it is only practical with large baits such as breadpaste or luncheon meat. Large, wary carp, which would drop the bait if they felt the resistance of any added weight, are often fooled by a freeline leger.

small shot

bait provides weight

SSG or AA shot

The shot link leger rig is used for fishing at close range on clear canals and small rivers.

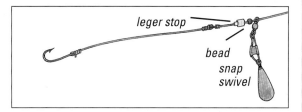

leger stop

bead
snap
swivel

The running leger with bomb is a good basic system for fishing a groundbaited area.

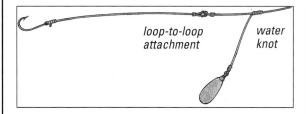

loop-to-loop attachment

water knot

The fixed link leger with bomb is a streamlined, sensitive rig designed to present the bait when there's a soft, silty lake bed. The bomb sinks into the silt but leaves the line exposed.

FEEDERS

If fish are not very active in your swim, use a feeder to lay groundbait to attract fish around the hookbait. There are two basic types: open-end and block-end feeders. The open-end cage feeder, made from latticed metal, can literally be buried in a ball of groundbait laced with maggots or casters and cast into the fishing area. Once in the water the groundbait mix crumbles away, leaving the feeder frame which offers little resistance when a fish is hooked or when the rig is retrieved.

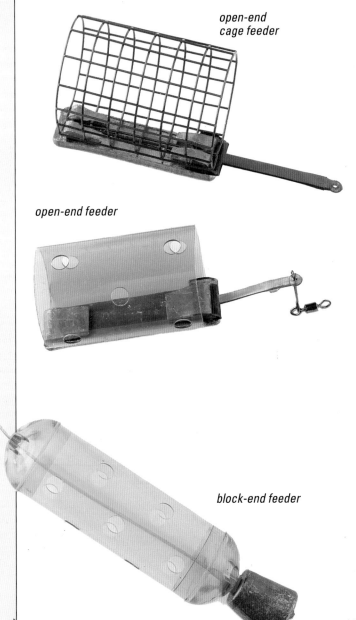

open-end
cage feeder

open-end feeder

block-end feeder

SWIMFEEDER RIGS

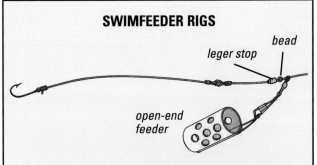

bead

leger stop

open-end
feeder

The open-end feeder rig is a favourite for laying down an area of groundbait and hook samples, which are packed into the feeder for every cast.

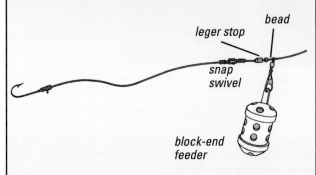

bead

leger stop

snap
swivel

block-end
feeder

The block-end feeder is filled with maggots which escape gradually into the swim. It can be replaced quickly with a bomb if the fish start to feed heavily.

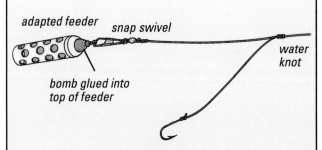

adapted feeder

snap swivel

water
knot

bomb glued into
top of feeder

With the weight directly on the end of the line, the long range paternoster rig gives long casts. The bite registers immediately on the bite indicator (see right). Start with a feeder to top the swim up with food. If the fish start to feed well, the feeder can be changed to a less cumbersome bomb.

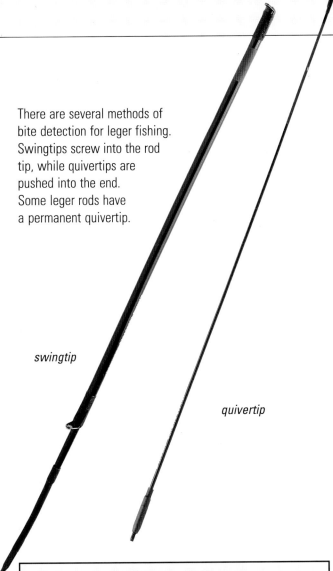

There are several methods of bite detection for leger fishing. Swingtips screw into the rod tip, while quivertips are pushed into the end. Some leger rods have a permanent quivertip.

swingtip

quivertip

THE QUIVERTIP

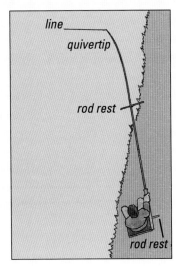

line
quivertip
rod rest
rod rest

The quivertip is probably the most popular form of bite detection for general legering. Cast out the tackle and let it settle on the bottom. Tighten the line, with the rod on the rests, until the quivertip is slightly flexed.

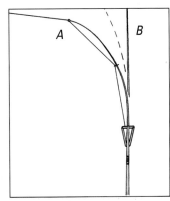

A   B

If the tip bends toward A, the fish is moving away from you. Movement B shows it is moving towards you. In both cases, strike immediately.

BUTTS AND BOBBINS

Two other devices for showing leger bites are butt and bobbin indicators. To make a simple bobbin, clip the cap from a detergent bottle on the line, or use a piece of bread paste. Strike when A or B occurs.

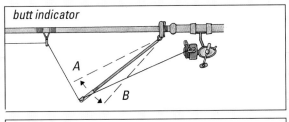

butt indicator

A

B

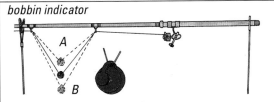

bobbin indicator

A

B

THE SWINGTIP

The swingtip is another leger bite detector - but it can only be used when the water is still.

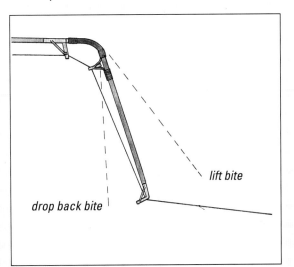

lift bite

drop back bite

POLE FISHING

WHY A POLE?

A pole will enable you to present your bait with a delicacy and accuracy that is difficult with a rod and reel. It is also a very quick method of bringing in small fish. This is invaluable during competitions, when the winner is the angler who catches the greatest weight of fish in the time allowed.

Start with a 7-8m pole on a familiar canal or lake with plenty of small fish. There you can practise unshipping the sections while bringing in fish.

A pole is simply lots of rod-like sections that can be joined to give the angler a very long reach. Using a full-length 11m pole can seem a daunting prospect, but you will be surprised at the speed and other benefits of the method.

A pole is made up of sections. The most comfortable way to hold it while waiting for a bite is to rest it on your knee.

Pole floats are very light and delicate. They are attached to the line through an eye on the body of the float, and also by a sleeve pushed onto the float's stem. An extra sleeve might be needed for neat presentation of a large-bodied float.

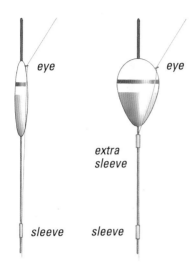

eye

eye

extra sleeve

sleeve

sleeve

There are three basic shapes of pole float: slim, body down and body up. Some have wire stems which provide greater stability for fishing in disturbed water.

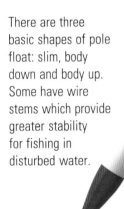

slim

body down

body up

FLICK TIP

There's no reel with a pole - instead, the line is connected directly to the tip by one of two methods. The simplest, called a flick tip, is a fine length of solid carbon or glass fibre which is connected to the top joint. A small loop at the end provides a connecting point for the line. A flick tip gives a lightning-fast strike, needed for the tentative or choosy bites of small fish.

POLE ELASTIC

The second method is designed for larger fish. It consists of a length of pole elastic threaded through the top two sections of pole. This acts as a shock absorber when a fish is hooked, lessening the force which would otherwise be borne by the main line or hooklength.

Pole elastic is colour coded - here is a guide to breaking strains and a suitable hooklength to use with each one:

Colour	Breaking strain	Hooklength
White	12oz/340g	5-10oz/140-280g
Red	1lb/0.45kg	10-14oz/280-400g
Green	1.25lb/0.56kg	12oz-1.1lb/340-500g
Blue	2.25lb/1kg	1.1lb-1.7lb/0.5kg-0.8kg
Black	3lb/1.4kg	1.7lb-2.6lb/0.8-1.2kg
Yellow	4lb/1.8kg	2.6lb-3.2lb/1.2-1.6kg

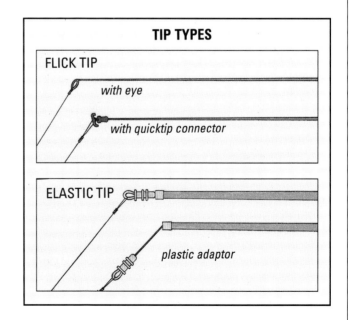

TIP TYPES

FLICK TIP

with eye

with quicktip connector

ELASTIC TIP

plastic adaptor

43

WEIGHTS

Where any bulk weight is needed, usually with body-down or body-up floats, weights called Olivettes are usually the best choice. Smaller weights below the Olivette can be provided by small weights called 'styls', or by small shot.

THE CORRECT WEIGHT

You can buy pole rigs already assembled, with the correct weight attached to the line. If you assemble your own rigs, it is best to add the heavier weights first. Fine adjustments to the float's setting can then be made by adding styl weights or shot.

Olivette weights are simply threaded on the line and can be held in place with a tiny shot. Styl weights clamp over the line and should be fixed into place with special pincers.

styl pincers

Olivette

styl weights

POLE RIGS

Rigs for pole fishing consist of a length of main line, a hooklength, weights and a float. A 12oz bs hooklength of about 18in, double looped to a main line of 1-1.5lb, will be quite enough for most smaller fish. Where larger fish are expected, in weedy swims, 1.7lb connected to 2.6lb would be more appropriate. Have a selection of size 18 to 24 hooks to use with baits such as bread punch and maggots.

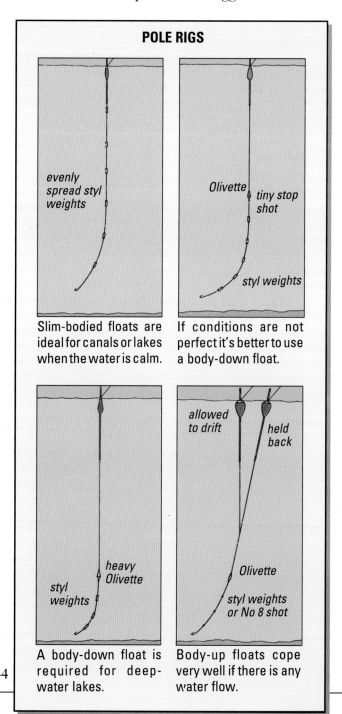

POLE RIGS

evenly spread styl weights

Olivette *tiny stop shot*

styl weights

Slim-bodied floats are ideal for canals or lakes when the water is calm.

If conditions are not perfect it's better to use a body-down float.

styl weights *heavy Olivette*

allowed to drift *held back*

Olivette *styl weights or No 8 shot*

A body-down float is required for deep-water lakes.

Body-up floats cope very well if there is any water flow.

44

CASTING

Casting, or putting in, can be done in two main ways. When a short length of pole is being used, the tackle can be swung out under the pole. If there is a stiff beeze, an overhead cast may be necessary.

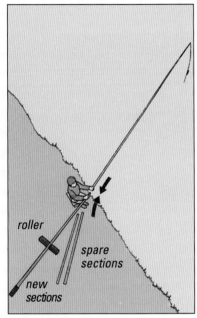

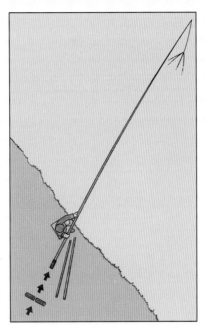

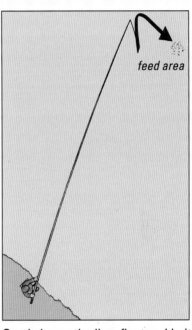

feed area

With a long pole, add new sections to the butt end. A pole roller will allow you to attach and unship several sections at once.

Carefully push out the pole until you've added enough sections to reach the feed area.

Gently lower the line, float and bait into the feed area.

It's best to assemble pole rigs at home, because it's a fiddly job. Assembled rigs should be wound on to a winder and held in position with a nylon clip or a pole rig anchor, where they will stay neat and tidy.

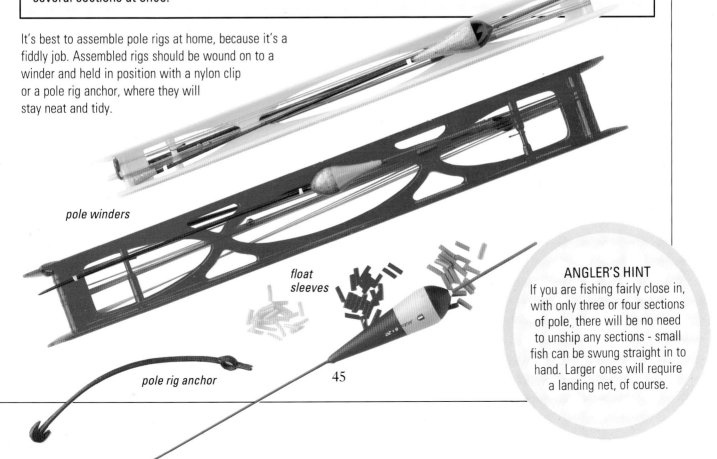

pole winders

float sleeves

pole rig anchor

ANGLER'S HINT
If you are fishing fairly close in, with only three or four sections of pole, there will be no need to unship any sections - small fish can be swung straight in to hand. Larger ones will require a landing net, of course.

FISHING FOR PREDATORS

Predatory fish, such as pike, zander, perch and large trout, are the tigers of the river. They have needle-sharp teeth and fight ferociously, so you'll have a *real* fight on your hands when you hook one of these voracious hunters. Get your catch close to the bank, and it'll fight even harder!

TACKLE

Use a 11ft (3.3m) specimen rod, with a test curve of at least 2½lb, to cope with these fierce, heavy fish and the larger baits needed. Your fixed-spool reel should have a deep spool loaded with 200m of 10-12lb line. Only perch can be caught safely on a lighter rod and line because they seldom grow to more than 3-4lb.

You'll need a wire trace, or leader, instead of a nylon hooklength, so your prey doesn't bite through the line. Also, use a landing net with large, 1m, triangular arms and a deep mesh.

FISHING A BAIT

Freeline legering (see page 38) is the simplest method of bait fishing for large predators. It uses only bait mounted on treble hooks. When you have cast out, leave the bale arm open and wait for the bait to settle on the bottom. You will know this has happened when the line goes slack.

Place the rod on a couple of rests. The front rest can be an electronic bite indicator, which will emit a bleeping noise when a fish moves off with the bait. The set-up (shown in the diagram above) will be more sensitive if a simple bobbin or 'monkey climb' indicator is used, too. The 'monkey climb' bobbin moves up and down a pole and so is less affected by wind. Leave the bale arm open so that when a fish takes the bait there will be no resistance to cause it to drop the bait.

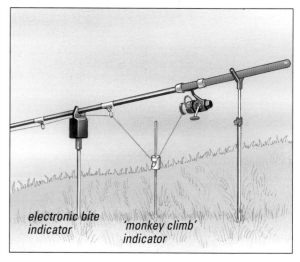

FREELINE LEGER INDICATORS

electronic bite indicator

'monkey climb' indicator

Predatory fish, especially pike and large perch, do not hunt in open water. Instead, they lie in wait in reeds and other underwater growth, ready to ambush any prey which swims within striking distance. Depressions in the lake or river bed also make ideal ambush points.

bay

submerged willows

MAKING A TRACE

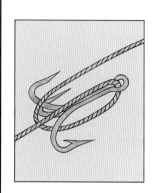 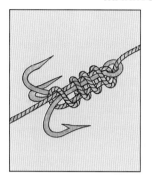 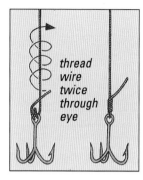 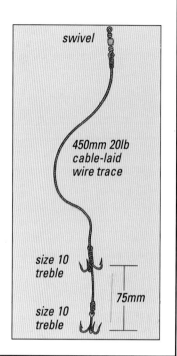

To make a trace for fishing a medium to large bait, thread the end of a 450mm length of cable-laid wire through the eye of a size 10 treble hook and push the hook along the wire about 100mm.

Wrap the wire four times around the shank and back through the eye. Now put a cork or polystyrene over the hook points so you don't injure yourself while you add a second hook.

Take another size 10 treble hook and fasten it to the end. Trim off the tag end of wire with wire cutters. Fasten a swivel to the other end of the wire, using the same method of attachment as for the bottom hook.

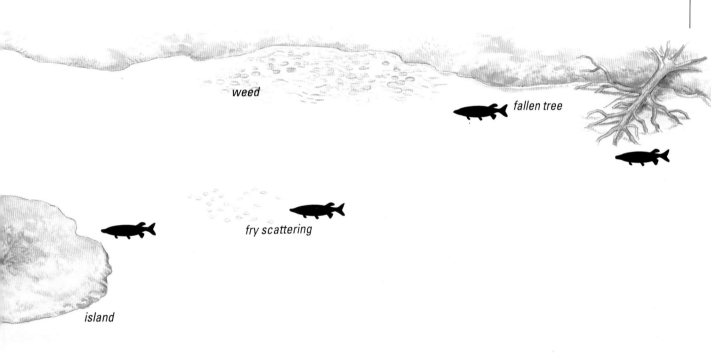

weed

fallen tree

fry scattering

island

rushes

FISH BAITS

Predatory fish feed mainly on other fish, so a dead fish bait will be the most effective. You can buy it from a fishmongers - sprats, herrings and mackerel are all good baits.

Alternatively, devote a session to catching bait, then keep it in a freezer until you need it. Whole baits of about 125mm in length are ideal for pike and zander, although smaller ones are better for perch. Freshwater baits should be killed humanely as soon as they are caught. Thankfully the cruel practice of using live fish as bait is becoming less common.

FLOAT PATERNOSTERS

The float paternoster (shown on the next page) is a relatively elaborate rig, designed for fishing a lake bed covered with weed. The bait is suspended above the bottom and so is more easily seen by a predator. This method is particularly suitable for catching zander, which are at home in murky conditions, whereas pike prefer clearer water.

WOBBLED BAITS

If you prefer to be more active, cast and then retrieve the bait using the reel. The bait will wobble in the water, like a swimming fish, and will attract the predator. The method is best suited to a lake which has lots of shallow bays and inlets, or a river. Vary the speed of retrieve and also the depths at which you fish the bait.

MOUNTING DEADBAITS

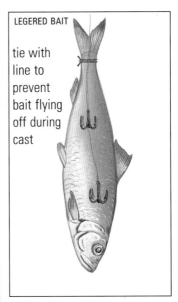

LEGERED BAIT

tie with line to prevent bait flying off during cast

HALF FISH LEGERED BAIT

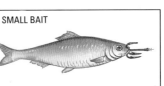

SMALL BAIT

WOBBLE BAIT

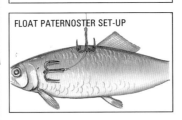

FLOAT PATERNOSTER SET-UP

A magnificent river pike - a fearsome predator.

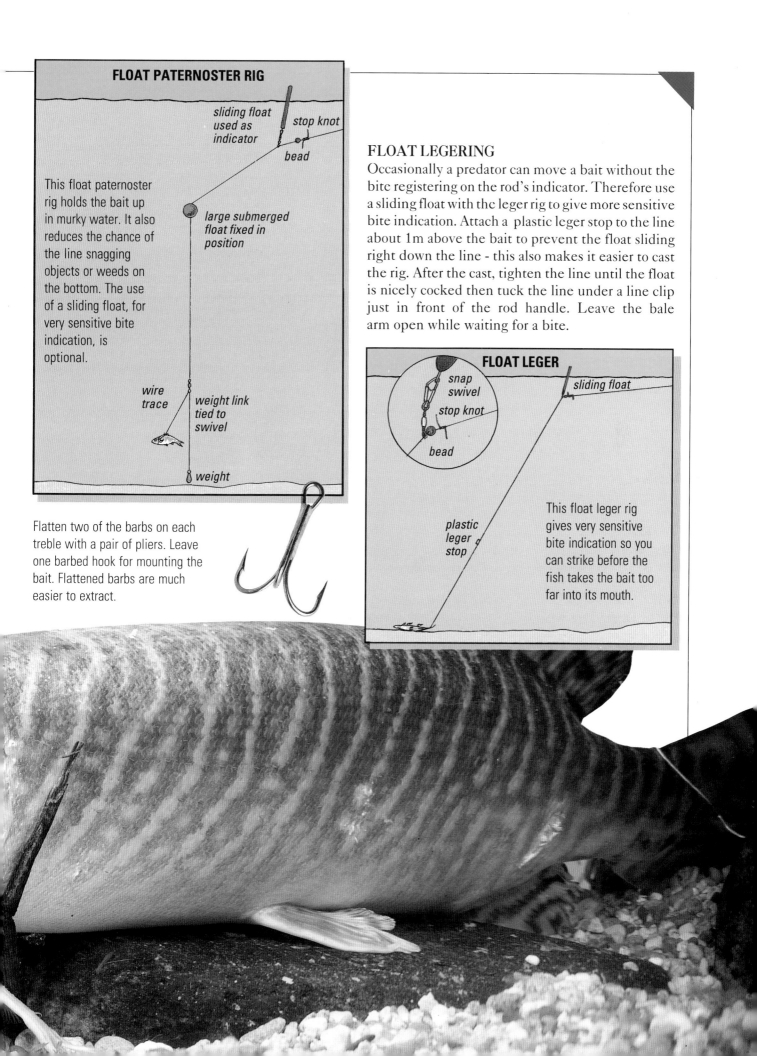

FLOAT PATERNOSTER RIG

sliding float used as indicator

stop knot

bead

This float paternoster rig holds the bait up in murky water. It also reduces the chance of the line snagging objects or weeds on the bottom. The use of a sliding float, for very sensitive bite indication, is optional.

large submerged float fixed in position

wire trace

weight link tied to swivel

weight

Flatten two of the barbs on each treble with a pair of pliers. Leave one barbed hook for mounting the bait. Flattened barbs are much easier to extract.

FLOAT LEGERING

Occasionally a predator can move a bait without the bite registering on the rod's indicator. Therefore use a sliding float with the leger rig to give more sensitive bite indication. Attach a plastic leger stop to the line about 1m above the bait to prevent the float sliding right down the line - this also makes it easier to cast the rig. After the cast, tighten the line until the float is nicely cocked then tuck the line under a line clip just in front of the rod handle. Leave the bale arm open while waiting for a bite.

FLOAT LEGER

snap swivel

stop knot

bead

sliding float

plastic leger stop

This float leger rig gives very sensitive bite indication so you can strike before the fish takes the bait too far into its mouth.

SPINNERS, SPOONS AND PLUGS

Perch, pike, zander, trout and bass all respond to artifical baits, or lures. If you do not want to wait for a predator to pick up your static fish bait, especially during colder weather, then this active method is well worth trying.

ON THE MOVE

Mobility is the key with lure fishing. All you really need is your rod, landing net and a bag. Carry an assortment of lures (in a lure box, so you don't hook yourself), a soft gardening glove and artery forceps for removing hooks, an assortment of swivels and a few anti-kink vanes or weights. Also carry a pair of pliers for running repairs to your tackle.

RODS AND REELS

Rods for lure fishing (called spinning rods) have large-diameter line guides to give better casting. Choose a rod with hard-wearing guides that can withstand the constant rubbing of the line. If the rod feels right - be it 7ft, 8ft or 9ft (2.1m, 2.4m or 2.7m) - that's the one for you. However, a longer rod is useful when there are reeds between you and the water.

A fixed-spool reel with 6lb line can be used with small lures where the fish don't run very big, but you'll need 10-12lb line where larger predators lurk.

SWIVEL AND TWIST

Wire lure traces have a swivel on one end and a snap swivel on the other. The snap swivel is the connecting point for the lure, allowing it to be changed in seconds.

Line twist can be a problem, especially with a rotating lure. You can overcome it by attaching an anti-kink vane to the line just above the top swivel. The vane acts like a keel when the lure is retrieved, cutting straight through the water and forcing the swivel to function properly as the lure turns.

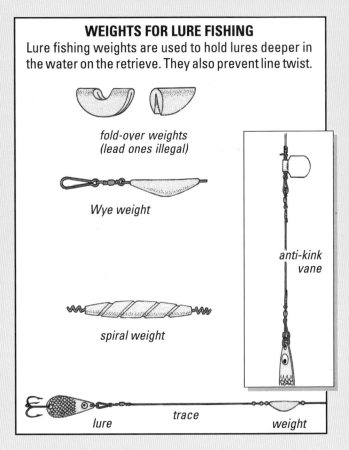

WEIGHTS FOR LURE FISHING
Lure fishing weights are used to hold lures deeper in the water on the retrieve. They also prevent line twist.

fold-over weights (lead ones illegal)

Wye weight

spiral weight

anti-kink vane

lure   trace   weight

Lures mimic real fish. Spinners revolve as they are dragged through the water, while spoons, such as the famous 'Toby' design, wriggle and wobble like a wounded fish. Then there are plugs, fascinating creations developed in the USA. Some plugs skitter along the surface when retrieved, others float on the surface when stationary and dive when retrieved.

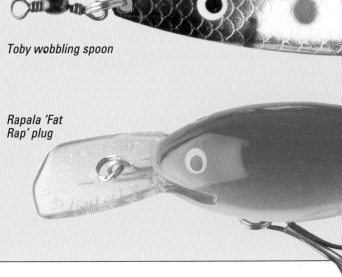

Toby wobbling spoon

Rapala 'Fat Rap' plug

very steep dive   *shallow dive*   *on or near surface*

Some plugs have an adjustable diving vane, on the nose, to set the diving motion.

ABU Droppen spinner

Rapala jointed plug

A short spinning rod is easier to handle in a boat. Many good river pike will be found almost under the bank, out of the main current. Cast downstream then work the lure back toward you.

VARYING THE RETRIEVE

current

A lure retrieved erratically, similar to a wounded fish, is far more tempting than one drawn evenly through the water. Turn the reel handle, then suddenly stop so the lure sinks for a few seconds, with a fluttering motion, before retrieving again.

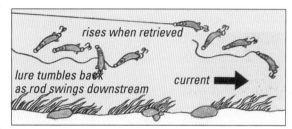

rises when retrieved

lure tumbles back as rod swings downstream   *current*

The river current can also be used to tumble a sunk lure. Stop retrieving and swing the rod tip downstream before resuming the retrieve.

SEA FISHING

What's the attraction of sea fishing? There's fabulous scenery, you don't need a rod licence, and the fish taste great! However, success in sea fishing, whether from the shore or a boat, depends a lot on a knowledge of the tide. Buy a tide table so you will know when the water is high, the best time for fishing, or when it's low, the best time for gathering bait.

STAY WARM AND DRY

Suitable clothing is extremely important. Always carry extra sweaters and a woolly hat in case you feel your body temperature dropping. Waders are ideal for beach fishing, but rope-soled yachting shoes are better suited to slippery boat decks. Neoprene mittens will keep your hands warm - and a quick wring when they become wet will soon dry them.

THE BEACHCASTER

For fishing from a beach you will need a beachcaster, a powerful rod capable of casting long distances. Choose one as large as you can comfortably hold. Make sure it's designed for use with a fixed-spool reel and has a large line guide on the bottom section.

REEL AND LINE

A fixed-spool reel for sea fishing is easier to use than a multiplier (see page 60) and will produce long, trouble-free casts. Buy a carbon model with stainless steel bearings, to resist saltwater corrosion; it should accomodate at least 200m of 15lb line.

A 15lb line is adequate for open, sandy beaches, but in rocky areas something stronger is needed. In any case, tie 10m of heavier line to the front end of the main line as a safety precaution. This 'shock leader' will prevent the weight snapping off during the cast. Increase the shock leader's strength for heavier casting weights, eg 3oz weight - 30lb leader; 4oz weight - 40lb; 5oz weight - 50lb, and so on.

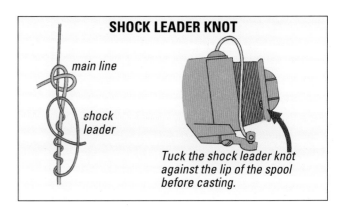

SHOCK LEADER KNOT

main line

shock leader

Tuck the shock leader knot against the lip of the spool before casting.

Although you will be close to the water's edge when fishing from a beach, it is best to keep the bulk of your equipment some way back from the rising tide, out of harm's way.

ANGLER'S HINT
Always go fishing with an adult. Make sure a rising tide won't cut off your fishing position, and never fish from rocks when the sea is very rough.

LARGE HOOKS

Large hooks come in a variety of designs, or patterns. The finer hooks like the Aberdeen are used for flatfish such as flounders and dab; heavier ones like the O'Shaughnessy are required for powerful fish such as cod or wrasse. You must use non-corrosive sea hooks for sea fishing.

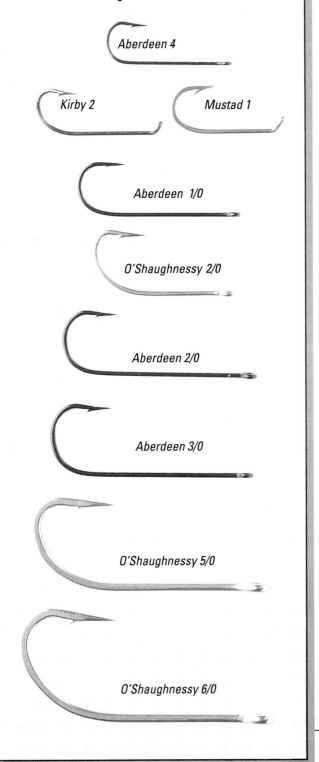

Aberdeen 4

Kirby 2

Mustad 1

Aberdeen 1/0

O'Shaughnessy 2/0

Aberdeen 2/0

Aberdeen 3/0

O'Shaughnessy 5/0

O'Shaughnessy 6/0

AN OFF-THE-GROUND CAST

There are several ways of casting from the shore, some of them quite complicated and requiring special rods. This off-the-ground cast is suitable for a standard beachcaster. Always tighten the reel clutch completely before making a cast, and make sure that no-one is standing close to you.

line trapped

bale arm open

direction of cast

Stand almost side on to the direction of the cast. Turn your body to hold the rod behind you, keeping your weight on your back foot. Rest the bait on the ground. Wear a protective finger glove to protect your forefinger during the cast.

Pull the rod forward across your chest, turning forward as you do. You should begin to transfer your weight towards your front foot.

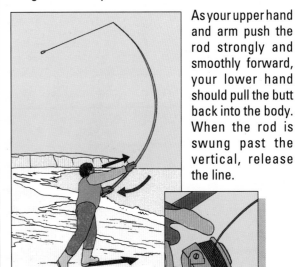

As your upper hand and arm push the rod strongly and smoothly forward, your lower hand should pull the butt back into the body. When the rod is swung past the vertical, release the line.

SHORE FISHING

There are not many places along the shore which are without fish. Beaches, rocks, harbour walls, jetties and piers are all worth exploring with a rod and line. However, the fish are not evenly distributed along the coast, and what may be a good venue one day may yield very little the next. Plan your fishing trip carefully, taking account of the tides and weather, to get the most from your visit to the shore.

FINDING THE FISH

Fish will be found where there's food. A gently-sloping beach will provide rich pickings for bass just after a storm, when the breakers have exposed such delicacies as lugworms and razorfish. During calm weather the bass might be feeding elsewhere, amongst rocks. Fishing from a pier or jetty might produce nothing on a small tide but could provide non-stop action when the water is high on a spring tide.

Summer, from May onwards, is the best time of year to cast a bait from the shore, when many species move close to the shoreline. They also swim up estuaries and creeks in search of food. Good shore fishing can also be had in the winter as shoals of cod move inshore, though night fishing usually accounts for the bigger catches.

This huge conger eel was caught near a harbour wall, where there are many feeding opportunities for fish. When you arrive at a beach, just prior to the tide coming in, position your base so you will be casting into a feature such as a gulley between fingers of rock. When it is covered by the rising tide, this bit of the sea bed will trap food and become a restaurant for fish.

Use a rod rest when bites are scarce, and to hold your rod and reel clear of sand when you change bait or tackle. A monopod is suitable for firm, sandy beaches, while the bulkier tripod is designed for shingle beaches, rocks and harbour walls.

ANGLER'S HINT
Thread a couple of coloured plastic beads on the line, just above the hook, as an added attraction for fish - it really works!

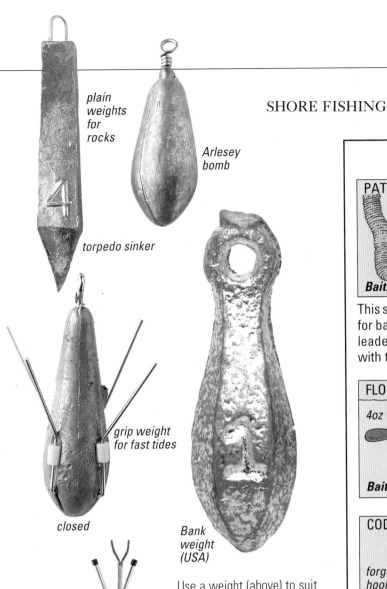

plain weights for rocks

Arlesey bomb

torpedo sinker

grip weight for fast tides

closed

Bank weight (USA)

Use a weight (above) to suit the conditions. Calm water can be tackled with 3oz or 4oz weights; 5oz or 6oz ones will be adequate for most open beaches. Strong-running tides may require even 8oz grip weights to hold the bait on the bottom. A firm tug will open the grips so it can be retrieved.

RIGS

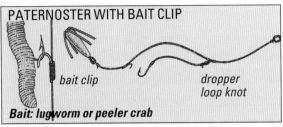

PATERNOSTER WITH BAIT CLIP

bait clip

dropper loop knot

Bait: lugworm or peeler crab

This simple rig is ideal for casting from an open beach for bass. A clip will hold the bait neatly alongside the leader during the cast, but will release it on impact with the water.

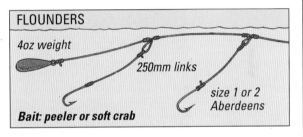

FLOUNDERS

4oz weight

250mm links

size 1 or 2 Aberdeens

Bait: peeler or soft crab

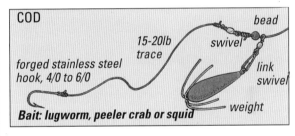

COD

bead

15-20lb trace

swivel

forged stainless steel hook, 4/0 to 6/0

link swivel

weight

Bait: lugworm, peeler crab or squid

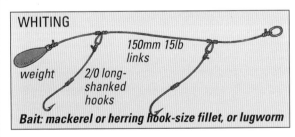

WHITING

150mm 15lb links

weight

2/0 long-shanked hooks

Bait: mackerel or herring hook-size fillet, or lugworm

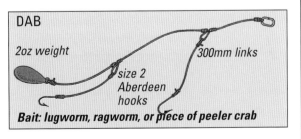

DAB

2oz weight

300mm links

size 2 Aberdeen hooks

Bait: lugworm, ragworm, or piece of peeler crab

FISHING FROM ROCKS

It is not always necessary to hurl a bait far out to sea in order to catch a decent-size fish. During warm weather you might look down from a rocky perch or jetty and see large fish swimming below. They could be mullet, browsing amongst the weed, or bass looking for prawns. Even a shoal of mackerel could suddenly appear right beneath your feet as they herd frantic sandeels before them.

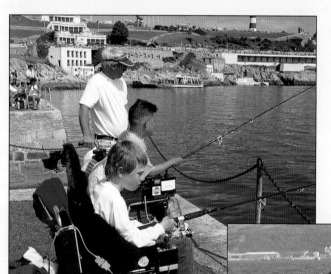

You don't have to go onto a beach or rocks to find exciting fishing. Jetties and harbour walls are ideal sites for anglers with limited mobility.

Get a friend to use a strong, large-meshed landing net to land large fish from a steeply-sloping gravel beach or other difficult situation. Use a long-handled net when fishing from rocks - it's just too dangerous leaning over the water to grab a fish by hand.

Where you are some way above the water, have a drop net ready to hoist up fish of 1lb or more. Always secure the rope to a bollard or rail.

HARBOURS

Interesting fishing can often be had in the shelter of harbours, especially when fishing boats are unloading their catch - again, you will often find fish directly beneath your rod. The two hours each side of high tide will often provide the most action, especially during a spring tide.

A beachcaster is too cumbersome for harbour fishing. Use something with a more sensitive tip, such as a spinning or carp rod. Line can also be lighter - 8lb to 10lb should be adequate. Light float fishing is the best method, as it keeps the bait off the bottom, away from greedy shore crabs.

ESTUARIES

Further up the estuary, flounders can provide non-stop action at high tide as they move out of the main river channel and over the submerged flats in search of food. Pieces of shore crab are the ideal bait for these flatfish - and, unfortunately, for shore crabs, too. Fix a piece of buoyant material, such as balsa wood, just above the bait to lift it clear of the crabs' grabbing nippers.

Once again, long casts are seldom needed. A 10lb line, used with a light beachcaster or a specimen rod, will be quite strong enough.

SNAGS

Snagging the bottom is a problem when fishing among rocks, so attach the weight to the main line with a link of lower breaking strain line. If your weight becomes snagged, point the rod straight at the snag and pull steadily to break the weaker line. Your rig will be intact minus only the weight.

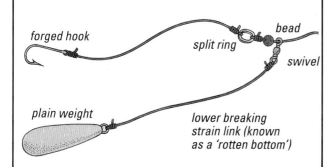

forged hook

bead

split ring

swivel

plain weight

lower breaking strain link (known as a 'rotten bottom')

FLOAT FISHING

This is very effective in rocky areas. Predators such as pollack and wrasse are attracted to the natural movement of the bait as it rises and falls with the sea. Also, there's less chance of snags if the float is holding the bait clear of underwater obstructions.

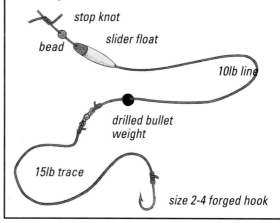

stop knot

slider float

bead

10lb line

drilled bullet weight

15lb trace

size 2-4 forged hook

Rocks provide a good vantage point for the angler. The best time is summer, when large bass can be found close in, especially when the top of the tide occurs at dawn or dusk.

Beware! The small weaver fish's spines (below) can inflict excruciating pain. This hideous creature lies half buried in the sand in shallow water, so always wear some protective footwear when wading in the water. If you happen to hook one, crush it immediately and dispose of it safely after cutting the line just above the hook.

BOAT FISHING

If you are lucky, you may have a relative or friend who is willing to take you out in their boat. Some very fine boat fishing can be had inshore, in sheltered estuaries and bays, rather than offshore, on the open sea. *Always* go with an adult companion who has experience with boats and is familiar with the area.

BOAT SENSE

Only go out in a properly-equipped dinghy, when the weather is sure to stay fine. Wear a life jacket at all times and, once afloat, *never* stand up in a small boat - everything can be done from a sitting position.

Always have a landing net on board when you are fishing from a dinghy. It is easy enough to swing small fish onboard, but don't risk lifting larger ones out with the rod. Also take a cushion because wooden boat seats are very uncomfortable.

FINDING THE FISH

As the tide rises in the estuary, fish will move in from the open sea. Bass, mullet and even mackerel can be encountered during the summer months. Bass are very partial to peeler crab so you might make contact with this splendid fish on flounder gear.

Mackerel will be visible as they chase shoals of small fry, causing the water surface to boil with activity. A lure such as a Toby or Mepps (see pages 50-51) cast across the front of the shoal will almost certainly produce a take. If you don't have a spare spinning rod already assembled, use a snap swivel to change, in seconds, to a shiny lure.

cast here

FISHING FOR FLOUNDERS

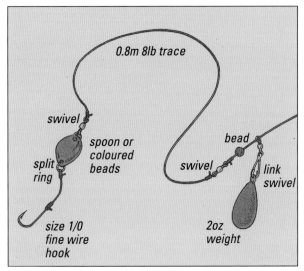

When fishing for flounders, tackle needs to be light - a spinning rod and fixed-spool reel loaded with 8-10lb line will be quite adequate.

Flounders respond well to a small spoon lure or a couple of coloured beads, just above the bait. These extra attractors move enticingly in the tide's flow.

If you see a shoal of mackerel moving up an estuary, cast and retrieve a lure across the shoal.

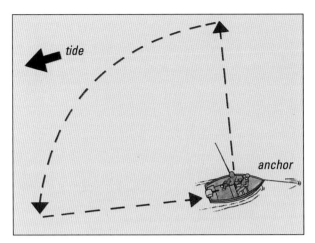

The tackle can be cast across the tide and and allowed to swing round in an arc, then retrieved very slowly.

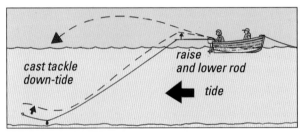

You can also cast directly down-tide. Raise and lower the tackle at intervals.

MULLET

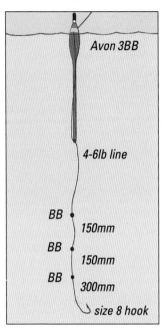

Avon 3BB

4-6lb line

BB — 150mm

BB — 150mm

BB — 300mm

size 8 hook

Estuary mullet are more cagey than the ones that feed in harbours. The best tackle for these 'grey ghosts' is a fresh-water float outfit baited with bread, white ragworm, fish pieces or maggots.

tide

A bait trail certainly produces more bites from mullet. Hang a cloth sack filled with a mixture of mashed fish heads and oily bits over the stern of the boat.

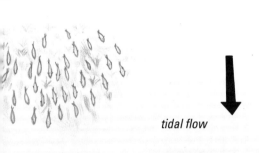

tidal flow

retrieve

direction of shoal

OFFSHORE BOAT FISHING RIGS

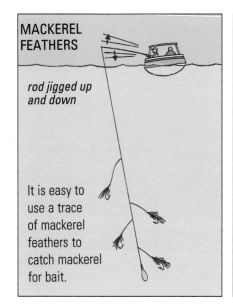

MACKEREL FEATHERS

rod jigged up and down

It is easy to use a trace of mackerel feathers to catch mackerel for bait.

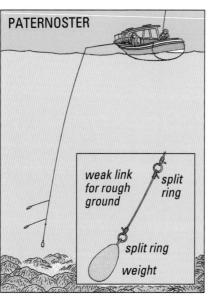

PATERNOSTER

weak link for rough ground

split ring

split ring

weight

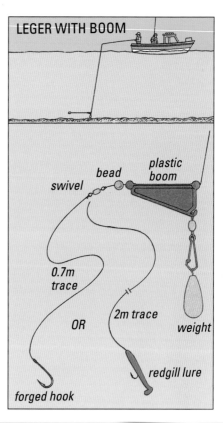

LEGER WITH BOOM

swivel

bead

plastic boom

0.7m trace

OR

2m trace

weight

forged hook

redgill lure

A paternoster is a simple rig. If your tackle tangles, use a leger rig with a plastic boom to hold the hook trace away from the main line. Both rigs are easy to use. Open the bale arm and let the weight sink to the bottom. Wind in line so the weight is just clear of the bottom. Strike when a fish takes the bait. With the redgill lure, retrieve the rig steadily. Predatory fish such as cod or pollack will hook themselves as they snatch the lure.

OFFSHORE BOAT FISHING

Licensed charter boats take anglers to offshore sites, called marks, that lie 8-15km out to sea. Rough ground is the favourite haunt of dogfish. Banks of gravel support a large variety of fish such as plaice, turbot, brill and bass. Banks of mud are feeding grounds for whiting, and reefs can be relied upon to produce pollack, coalfish and conger.

On the way out it is usual to slow down to catch mackerel for bait. This can be done using a trace of mackerel feathers. Sometimes there will be a mackerel on every feather, and enough bait can be caught in a very short time.

Multiplier reels are lighter than fixed-spool reels, and give a greater feeling of being in contact with the fish. However, line can come off the multiplier's drum too fast during casting, creating horrible tangles. Lots of practice and experience are needed before one can be used confidently.

EQUIPMENT

For offshore boat fishing you will need a powerful 7ft (2.4m) rod, coupled with a multiplier reel loaded with 200m of 20lb line.

A multiplier's drum can literally explode if the drag has been set too high and the reel used like a winch to bring a large fish up through several fathoms of water. Therefore set the drag correctly to yield line. Use the rod to take the strain as you use a slow up-and-down pumping action, reeling in slack line as the rod is lowered.

Sandeel lures (below) are used with leger rigs. Rubber squid (right), also known as 'Muppets', can be used on paternoster rigs.

sandeels

rubber squid

A charter boat will always have a good landing net aboard (left). If you decide to keep the fish to eat, kill it quickly with a sharp blow to the head with a 'priest' (below), a short, heavy metal bar.

priest

ANGLER'S HINT
Seasickness is often brought on by the cold. Have a good breakfast and then a couple of seasickness pills before a boat trip.

SEA FISHING BAITS

Although you can buy sea fishing baits from tackle shops, it is cheaper - and more fun - to collect them yourself. Provided it is stored properly, the bait will stay alive and healthy for a couple of days. Estuaries are often good bait hunting areas but they are dangerous if you don't leave well before the tide begins to rise. It is more sensible to search for bait along the foreshore. For example, open sandy beaches, close to the low water mark, provide good areas for lugworm. Only go bait hunting with an adult who knows the area well.

CRAB

Shore crabs that are casting, or losing, their old shell make an excellent bait for bass, flounders, plaice, dabs and cod. They can be found beneath weed-covered rock. Store them in a bucket with wet seaweed and cover the top with a towel saturated in sea water.

LUGWORM

These worms create their familiar casts near the low water mark on sand or mud beaches. Dig for them between the cast and the hole. Lugworms are a good bait for cod, whiting and bass. They are best used on the day you dig them, but will survive for a few days wrapped in newspaper.

RAGWORM

White ragworm, harbour or red rag, and the huge king rag, live in the unpleasant black mud in estuaries and close to harbours. White and red rag, used whole, make good bait for mullet and dabs. The king rag, best used in sections, is found in gravelly mud on the low water line. Its fierce nippers can inflict a painful bite, so grip it firmly right behind the head. Store ragworms in damp seaweed in a cool place. Remove any broken worms immediately or the whole ones will die.

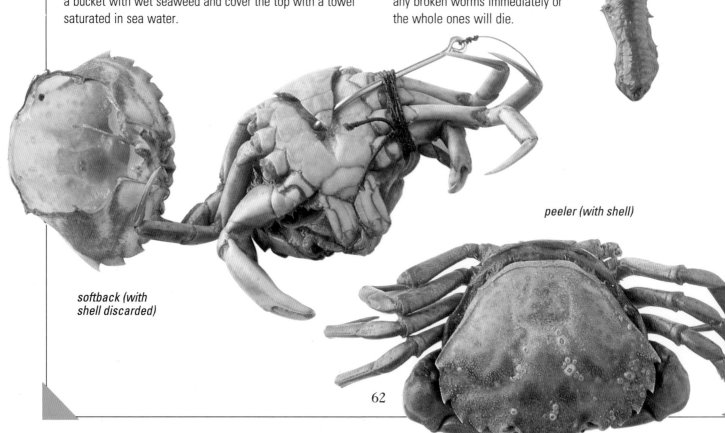

peeler (with shell)

softback (with shell discarded)

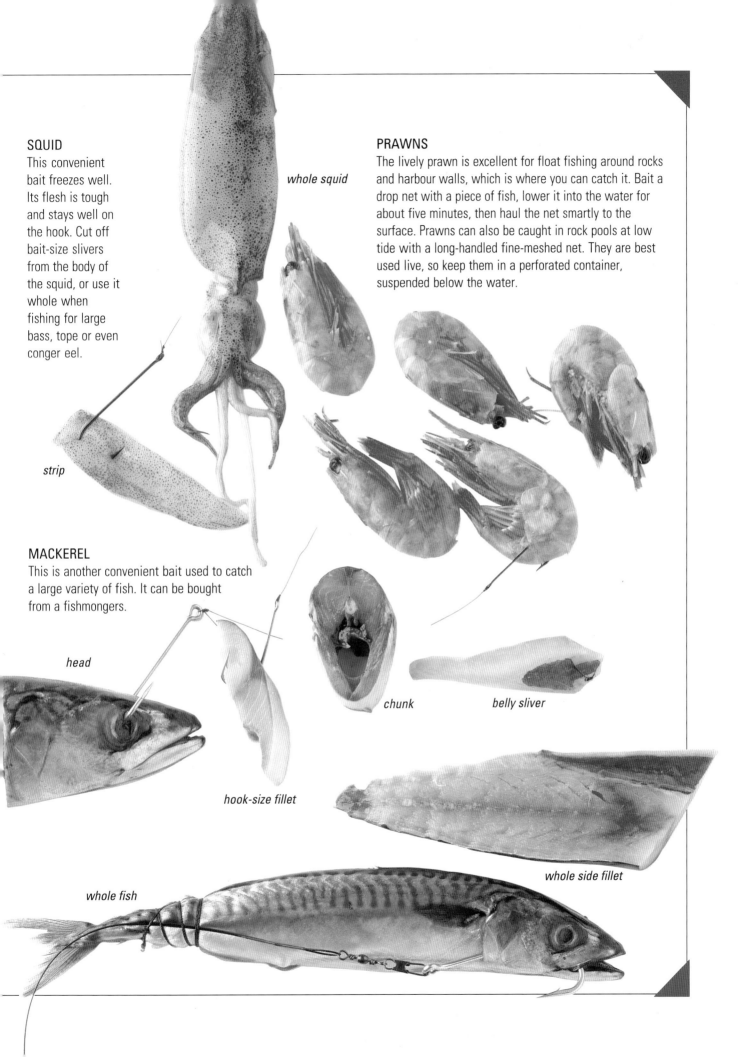

SQUID

This convenient bait freezes well. Its flesh is tough and stays well on the hook. Cut off bait-size slivers from the body of the squid, or use it whole when fishing for large bass, tope or even conger eel.

whole squid

strip

PRAWNS

The lively prawn is excellent for float fishing around rocks and harbour walls, which is where you can catch it. Bait a drop net with a piece of fish, lower it into the water for about five minutes, then haul the net smartly to the surface. Prawns can also be caught in rock pools at low tide with a long-handled fine-meshed net. They are best used live, so keep them in a perforated container, suspended below the water.

MACKEREL

This is another convenient bait used to catch a large variety of fish. It can be bought from a fishmongers.

head

chunk

belly sliver

hook-size fillet

whole side fillet

whole fish

FLY FISHING

Fly fishing is considered the most sporting method of angling. It uses an artificial 'fly' to imitate the insects or small fish that are the food of game fish such as trout. Fly fishing is easier than is commonly thought - it is only the method of casting that you might find difficult. You can teach yourself to cast, or learn from an experienced fly angler. Alternatively, pay for lessons with a professional instructor, who will provide tackle for the lessons.

The secret to successful fly fishing is presentation of the fly. Don't be distracted from learning good technique by the many flashy fly designs available.

ROD
Begin with a fly rod of about 8½ft (2.6m), suitable for casting a No 6 line. Look at the rod, just in front of the handle, for the letters AFTMA and a number or numbers. These indicate what line will perform most efficiently with the rod. A rod marked AFTMA 6 or AFTMA 5/7 (5, 6 or 7) will provide the right balance for the beginner.

REEL
A fly reel should be able to hold a 30yd (27m) fly line attached to backing line. Backing line is wound on to the reel first to provide a good bed for the main fly line, and for when a running fish strips all the fly line from the reel. Choose a reel with a standard size of spool, rather than a wide spool made to take heavier lines, eg No 7 up, and extra backing line.

LINE
There are two main types of fly line - called double taper (DT) and weight forward (WF). There are also lines that float and lines that sink, some very slowly and others quickly. A 'double taper No 6 floater' is best to start with: it falls lightly on the water and is also easy to lift off the surface for your next cast. The specification on the pack should read DT6F (double taper - 6 - floater).

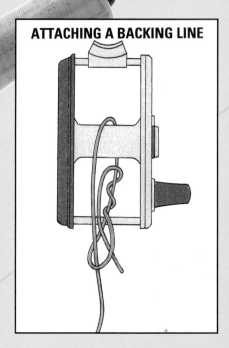

ATTACHING A BACKING LINE

Backing line comes on 50 or 75 metre spools and is tied to the reel as shown above. A braided leader butt (see page 66) makes a good connector between the backing and the line.

A moment of great excitement - hooking a fine trout. Now it has to be landed!

A correctly loaded reel. The line should lie clear of the reel's horizontal casing supports.

ANATOMY OF AN ARTIFICIAL FLY

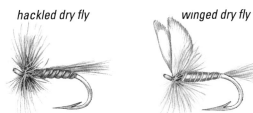

wings

body hackle

tail

shoulder hackle

body

ARTIFICIAL FLIES

hackled dry fly   *winged dry fly*

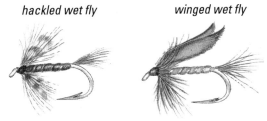

Dry flies imitate insects that are floating on the surface. They are made buoyant by applying a spray known as 'floatant' to the dressing.

hackled wet fly   *winged wet fly*

Wet flies are fished below the surface. They imitate drowned insects or, in the case of the more flashy patterns, small fish.

Nymphs are fished at various depths beneath the surface and imitate the stage before the aquatic insect emerges as an adult.

Lures and streamer flies are meant to give the impression of small fish. Many patterns look nothing like fish, but are, nevertheless, still effective.

main line

LEADERS

A leader is a link between the fly and the fly line. Level line can work quite well, but straighter, cleaner casts are produced with a tapered leader. The thicker end, or butt, is connected to the line and the finer end, the tippet, is tied to the fly. The most advanced leaders are made from braided nylon. These braided leaders are fairly expensive but give good casts. A nylon monofilament tippet will still have to be connected to the thin end of the braid, and changed from time to time, but the main part of the leader will last indefinitely.

Lengths cut from spools of 6lb, 4lb and 3lb fly leader monofilament line (below) can be tied together using the water knot to make a tapered leader. Cut a single length of line to make a tippet for a braided leader.

braided leader

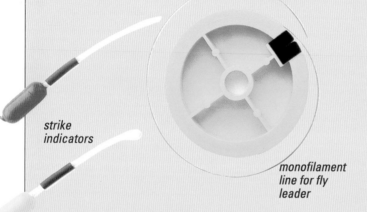

strike
indicators

monofilament
line for fly
leader

monofilament tippet

fly

CONNECTING A BRAIDED LEADER

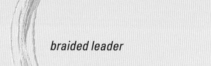

main line

braided leader

sleeve

butt

butt

braided
leader

loop-to-loop
attachment

monofilament
leader

fly   tippet

A reel with main line and leaders (above). Strike indicators (above left) are like miniature floats. They are attached to the leader and signal a take when a nymph is being fished.

66

LEARNING TO CAST

Learning to cast involves lots of practice. The object of the exercise is to throw a length of line straight out in front of you, onto the water surface. You will not need any water - a large lawn or field will do just as well. There is no need to connect the leader to the line when practising.

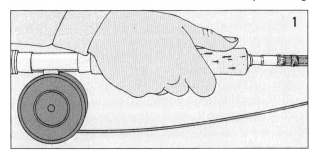

Grip the rod, with the thumb lying along the top of the handle and the reel hanging directly downwards.

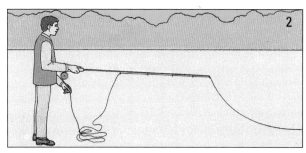

Hold the rod horizontally with about a rod length of line beyond the tip. Pull off some line from the reel.

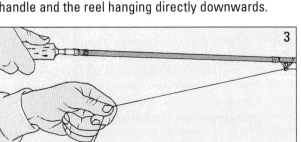

Hold the line with your free hand somewhere between the bottom line guide and the handle.

Lift the rod smartly from the horizontal to the vertical position and bring it to an abrupt stop. The line beyond the rod tip will sail back, up and behind you. Do not, on any back cast movement, allow the line to drop.

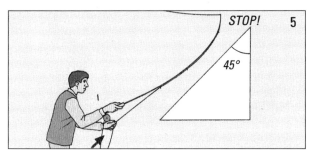

Drive the rod tip forward through 45° and again bring it to an abrupt stop while allowing some of the line, pulled from the reel, to slide from your free hand.

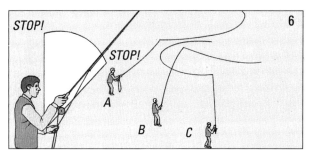

As the airborne line unrolls in front of you (A), grip once again with your free hand and bring the rod smartly back to the vertical position (B), and again bring it to an abrupt stop (C). (As you do this, imagine that you are standing with your back against a high brick wall.)

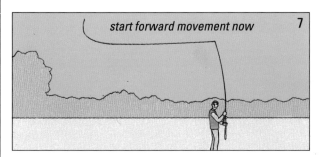

By now you should have extra airborne line, and it will be a help if you watch the line straightening out behind you. Start the forward movement just as the line is straightening out and before it begins to fall behind you.

Now, with enough line in the air, a final cast can be made. As the line unrolls in front of you again, release the grip of your free hand and the line will sail out to fall in a straight line.

FLY FISHING ON STILL WATERS

The many small fisheries that are stocked regularly with rainbow and brown trout provide the ideal place to start fly fishing. Many of them also contain very large trout, so it is a wise precaution to use a tippet of 6lb bs, going down to 4lb only if you are presenting a very tiny fly.

TIME FOR THE NYMPH

During the warmer months you will see fish swirling just beneath the surface. It is likely that they are feeding on ascending damselfly or sedge nymphs - and there are many imitations for situations like this.

Some artificial nymphs are weighted with lead wire and will sink fairly quickly to the bottom. When retrieved, the nymph starts to rise and give a realistic impression of the real creature swimming towards the surface. It is good practice to have a longer than normal leader - 4m or so - when fishing a nymph at depth, though it is less easy to control and will take some getting used to. Fish might take nymphs at any depth, so vary the depth of your retrieve until you find where they are feeding.

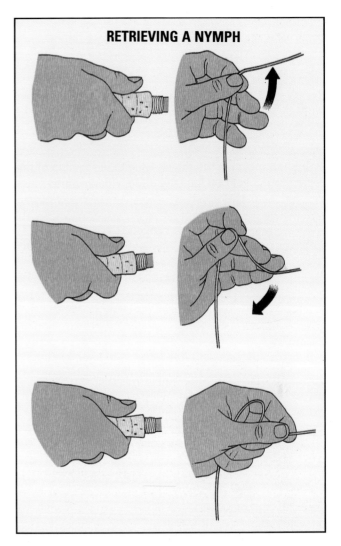

RETRIEVING A NYMPH

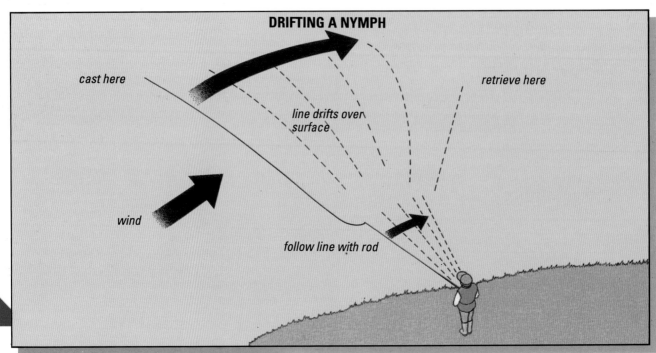

DRIFTING A NYMPH

cast here

retrieve here

line drifts over surface

wind

follow line with rod

Midge pupa, damselfly nymph and sedge pupa imitations, to name but a few, all work if presented correctly.

midge pupa

damselfly nymph

sedge pupa

HOW TO FISH THE MIDGE

Stillwater trout feed avidly where there is a concentration of midge pupae. These hang in the tension of the surface layer before turning into adult midges. A fine tippet is a must for fishing a midge. You should also apply floatant to the tippet.

Look for fish rising with the porpoise-like humping movement so typical of midge-eating trout. Drop your fly about 3m in front of a rising fish. If the fish stays on course it should see your fly and take it.

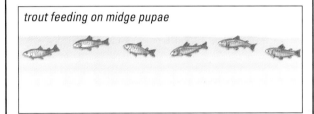

trout feeding on midge pupae

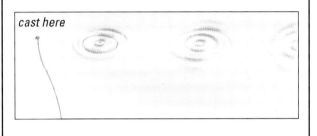

cast here

Don't be tempted to lift a fish out like this - the leader is likely to break. Always bring the fish to a net.

The water in many lakes is so crystal clear that the trout will only be deceived by an imitation tied to the finest tippet.

ANGLER'S HINT:
A short length of fluorescent drinking straw attached where the line joins the leader will make an easily visible bite indicator for when a trout takes a nymph.

WHEN TO USE A LURE

If there is no surface activity, usually when the weather is cold or when a bright sun shines high in the sky on a windless day, use a lure to arouse deep-lying, lazy trout. A sinking line is needed to keep the lure at a constant depth during the retrieve.

You will often see some anglers hauling lures back at incredible speeds, but a slow retrieve is often more productive - and cuts down on the number of tiring casts you have to make. Sometimes, as you retrieve, you will feel a fish plucking at the lure. Don't be tempted to jerk or make a half-hearted strike - just keep retrieving. If the trout is interested enough it will take the lure properly and usually hook itself.

Lures (below) can be used with a floating line when the trout are chasing fish fry at the end of the season. Cast into the disturbance and use an erratic 'wounded fish' retrieve. Ace of Spades, Missionary and Jersey Herd lures have all been designed to imitate fish fry.

Ace of Spades

Missionary

Jersey Herd

TIME FOR THE DRY FLY

If you see fish splashing on the surface near the shore, they are probably feeding on insects being blown onto the water. Cast a dry fly treated with floatant. Look on the bank upwind of the splashing for the insects you need to imitate. For example, hawthorn flies appear during May, beetles appear through the summer, and craneflies can be seen on the water at the end of summer and during autumn.

These are fly patterns, or designs, for deep lure fishing.

Viva

Orange Marabou

Yellow Mohican

Sweeney Todd

FLY FISHING ON STILL WATERS

When a trout takes your fly, wait for the line to start moving away before striking. If your fly is ignored, give it a twitch along the surface, because fish often snatch up struggling craneflies and skittering sedge flies. After catching a fish, always dry off the fly and re-treat it with floatant.

Any black imitation will work in a hatch of hawthorn flies - size being more important than accurate imitation. Use a dry fly with a fat body if beetles or ants are about. Craneflies have a unique shape so keep a couple of 'daddy-long-legs' imitations in your fly box, too.

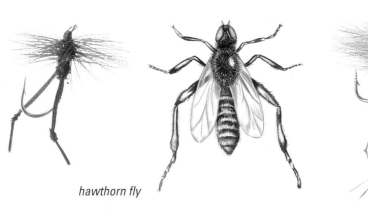

hawthorn fly

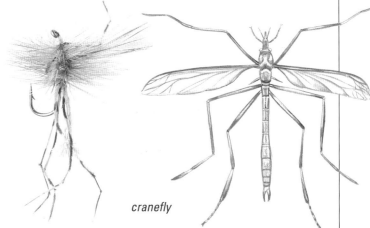

cranefly

FISHING FROM A BOAT

It is great fun fishing from a boat, but only go out with an adult who is experienced in using one. This is a purpose-built fly-fishing boat that is very stable so that the angler can stand in it. When netting a trout from a drifting boat, always bring the fish to the net on the windward side of the boat, to avoid drifting over the fish.

FLY FISHING ON RIVERS

STEALTH

Work your way upstream, so that you are approaching the fish from behind (trout always face upstream) and any vibrations from clumsy footfalls will tend to be carried downstream. Always move quietly and keep low - stealth is the name of the game.

WHAT FLY?

Trout living in wild streams are seldom fussy about what they eat. Any fly, beetle or caterpillar that falls on the water is eagerly grabbed. Hackled wet flies are the best sort to use when casting upstream because the soft hackles move enticingly with the current coming from behind. Winged wet flies are better for fishing downstream.

Sometimes only smaller fish will show any interest in a fly. A weighted nymph cast into the head of a pool will often tempt the deeper-lying larger fish.

Fishing on a twisty stream is very skilful sport. It demands great casting accuracy, although long casts are seldom required. You'll also need to master the side cast for where trees overhang the water. The principles are the same as the overhead cast - just lay the rod over and cast parallel to the water. In any event, always look behind you before casting to see if there are any obstructions which may snag you on the back cast.

You'll need only a small selection of flies. For dry flies try Grey Duster in sizes 16, 14 and 12 and Black Gnat in 16 and 14 (right). Your wet flies need only include Black Spider in 16, 14 and 12, and Black & Peacock Spider in 16 and 14 (below). A few size 14 or 12 weighted nymphs will also come in useful. Although looking nothing like a natural insect, the Cardinal is an example of a bright 'imitation' that can work in fast-flowing water.

Grey Dusters

Black Gnat

Cardinal

Black Spider

Black & Peacock Spider

Twinkle Orange (weighted nymph)

WHICH FISH?

If you see several fish rising in the same pool, cast to the best one. Small trout tend to make splashy rises in more open water, moving around as they do so. Larger trout seldom make much disturbance, and are difficult to spot as they rise in the shadow of over-hanging foliage. They will usually be in a choice position, called a larder, with a constant supply of insects borne on the current, and will rise in exactly the same spot time after time. If you spot a group of larger fish, cast to the downstream one first.

When you hook a fish, try not to let it run up the pool where it may spook other feeding fish. On a small, rough stream, some strong bullying will be required to keep a large trout clear of snags. In this sort of situation, using too fine a tippet on your leader is asking for trouble - fish no finer than 3lb, or 4lb if the stream is particularly snaggy.

PRESENTING A DRY FLY DOWNSTREAM

Where the banks are overgrown, you might have to cast downstream. The casting is not itself a problem, but it may be difficult to prevent the fly being dragged across the surface in an unnatural manner.

When casting to a fish which is downstream of you, make the fly fall just upstream of the fish. Attempt to introduce some slack as the line lands on the water.

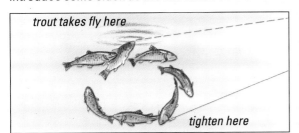

Wait until the trout has turned well down with the fly before striking.

PRESENTING THE FLY

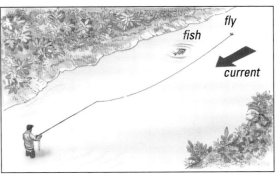

Cast your fly just upstream of a rising fish and allow it to float naturally downstream. Keep in touch with the fly by collecting slack line with your free hand, retrieving the line at the same speed as the current.

Wait until the fish has turned down with the fly before striking. If the fish rises to your fly but you fail to hook it, pause to see if it carries on feeding. If it does not you have probably 'put it down' and it is time to cast to the next fish upstream.

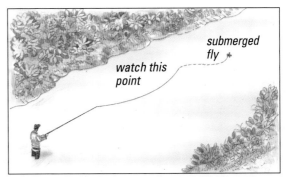

When you present a wet fly or a nymph, watch the end of the line and tighten to any suspicious move-ment. Quite often the fish will hook itself, especially in fast-running water.

SALTWATER FLY FISHING

The use of fly-type lures in conjunction with a fly rod and reel is a relatively new form of sea fishing, with the 'flies' imitating not insects but small fish, prawns or squid. It is practised mainly in the warmer waters of America, South Africa and Australia for fish such as barracuda, bonefish and tarpon. However, it also works in colder waters - bass, grey mullet, mackerel and sea trout can all be caught on fly fishing gear.

TACKLE
A No 8/9 rod, 9-10ft (2.7-3.0m) in length, with a fairly stiff action, is the ideal weapon for shore and boat work. The reel must be strong with a wide spool, loaded with as much backing line as it will comfortably accommodate. You'll need reels with sinking as well as floating lines available, so you can vary the depth of the retrieve. Braided leaders are best, and tippets should be 6-10lb monofilament.

This reel is ideal for saltwater fly fishing. It will hold plenty of strong line and backing. It is made of non-corrosive material and can cope with fast-running fish.

FISHING THE FLY
A spell of warm settled weather, with little or no wind, provides the ideal conditions for fly fishing for bass or mackerel as they feed on sandeels just off shore. Feeding activity is usually heralded by wheeling and diving gulls and terns. Approach the area in a dinghy, cutting the motor before you fish.

Bass and mackerel feeding in this manner will often be right on the surface, but the best specimens are usually swimming deeper, waiting for any dead or wounded fry to sink into their waiting jaws. A white and silver fly, tied to a 1/0 or 2/0 hook, will give a good impression of darting silver sandeels.

This huge fly is used for tarpon, a strong, skilful Atlantic game fish that can weigh as much as 90 kilograms.

Saltwater lures, such as these ones for American bonefish, are often made using reflective materials such as mylar and flashabou.

Grey mullet will often nose at fragments of weed, so a lure resembling seaweed might be their undoing. Try the silver-bodied Alexandra, which has green peacock feathers and a red tail as an added attraction. It was originally designed for sea trout, which often move upstream with mullet.

RETRIEVING

Where predatory fish are feeding near the surface, retrieve the fly just beneath the surface (A). Alternatively, let the fly sink (imitating a wounded or dead fry) - possibly catching a fish on-the-drop (B) - followed by a deep retrieve hoping to make contact with a deep-lying larger fish (C).

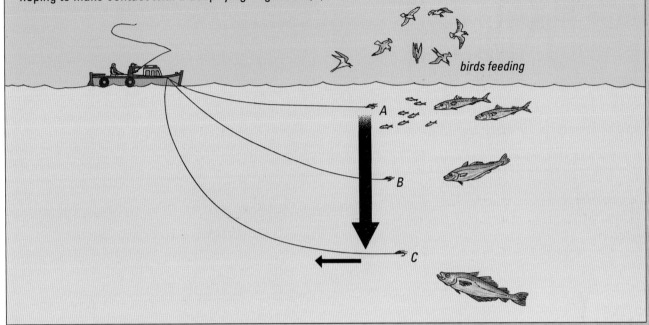

birds feeding

Some enormous fish can be caught on fly rod and reels - such as this magnificent American sailfish. The sailfish stuns its prey with its 'beak' before eating them.

ESTUARIES

A narrow estuary mouth is a favourite haunt of bass. Cast across the current with a sinking line, retrieving the fly at a fairly smart pace - and be prepared for the solid resistance of a hooked bass! You can try for mullet over shallow water further up the estuary, perhaps using a floating line so the fly doesn't snag the bottom.

ANGLER'S HINT
When fishing from rocks into deeper water, try to fish at different depths to find where the most fish are feeding.

INDEX

COD
L25-100cm, 2-20lb.
Shoals off most beaches October-March. Feeds on crustaceans and fish. Lugworm, crab or whole squid on size 4/0 hook, pirks.

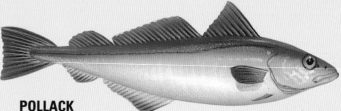

POLLACK
L30-100cm, 2-20lb.
Rough, rocky waters, June-February. Feeds on small fish, crustaceans and sandeels. Ragworm, mackerel, crab or squid on size 4/0 hook.

POUTING (BIB)
L15-40cm, 1-4lb.
Inshore, including rocky areas. Feeds on molluscs, shrimps and small fish. Ragworm or lugworm on size 1 hook, mackerel strip on size 1/0 or 2/0.

WHITING
L15-65cm, ½-5lb.
Inshore sandy sea beds, November to April; larger fish caught offshore. Feeds on or near bottom on crustaceans and small fish. Lugworm on size 1/0 hook, mackerel strip on size 2/0.

LING
L30-200cm, 2-30lb.
Young fish in shallow water, older fish in deep water, offshore. Feeds on small fish. Whole small mackerel or fillet on size 6/0 hook, pirks.

FLOUNDER
L15-50cm, 1-6lb.
Offshore banks, beaches and estuaries, November-February. Feeds on small fish and crustaceans. Peeler or soft crab on size 1/0 hook.

PLAICE
L20-70cm, ½-6lb.
Offshore banks and beaches, April-October. Feeds on worms and mussels on sea bottom. Lugworm or peeler crab on size 1 hook.

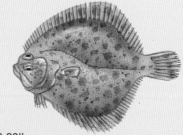

TURBOT
L20-90cm, 2-20lb.
Sandy sea bed; the largest specimens are from offshore banks. Feeds on small fish and crustaceans. Mackerel strip on 4/0 hook.

DAB
L20-50cm, ½-3lb.
Sandy sea beds and shallow bays, September-February. Feeds close to shore on worms on or near sea bottom. Piece of lugworm, ragworm or peeler crab on size 2 hook.

SOLE
L15-50cm, ½-3lb.
Sandy sea beds, shallow bays and estuaries in warmer waters, March-September. Feeds on worms and bivalves on sea bottom. Piece of lugworm or ragworm on size 2 hook.

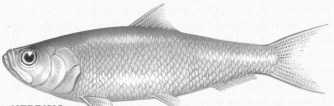

HERRING
L8-30cm, ½-1lb.
Mainly deep water. Feeds on plankton. Can be caught only on fine float tackle and small baits on size 14 or 16 hook: after dark is the best time.

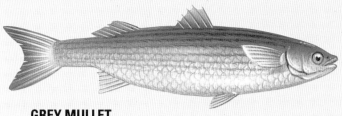

GREY MULLET
L20-75cm, 1-10lb.
Rocky shores, harbours and estuaries. Feeds on tiny organisms in mud and weed. White ragworm, bread flake or floating bread crust on size 8 hook, small artificial wet fly.

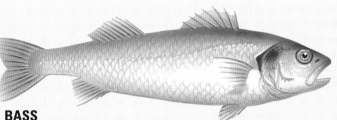

BASS
L30-100cm, 2-15lb.
Most beaches. Ferocious predator of small fish and sandeels. Peeler crab, mackerel, squid or lugworm on size 1/0-4/0 hook, artificial lures.

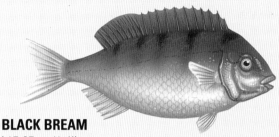

BLACK BREAM
L15-35cm, 1-4lb.
A warm-weather visitor to northern waters; prefers rocky areas and wrecks. Small hook-size fillets of mackerel on size 2 forged hook.

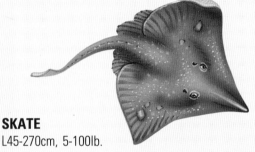

SKATE
L45-270cm, 5-100lb.
Deep waters. Feeds most actively in warmer months on fish and crabs and on sea bed. Whole mackerel or herring on size 8/0 hook.

LESSER SPOTTED DOGFISH
L45-80cm, 1½-3lb.
Usually over rough sea bed, April-November. Feeds mainly on bottom on fish and crustaceans. Lugworm on size 2/0 hook, whole squid, crab or fish strip on size 4/0.

MACKEREL
L15-50cm, ½-4lb.
All waters, May-September. Feeds on small fish and sandeels. Trace of small feathers, spinners, strips of fish on size 4 hook under sliding float rig.

BALLAN WRASSE
L15-50cm, 1-6lb.
Deep rocky inshore waters, often with thick seaweed, April-October. Feeds on molluscs and crustaceans. Ragworm or whole crab on size 2 forged hook.

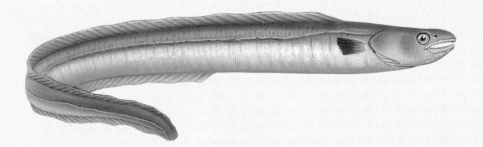

CONGER EEL
L60-250cm, 4-60lb.
Rocky coasts, harbour walls and offshore wrecks. Feeds on fish, crustaceans and squid. Whole squid or mackerel on size 8/0-10/0 hook.